The Rise of the Mediocracy

First published in 1975, *The Rise of the Mediocracy* is exhaustive, disturbing, devastating, yet often very funny. It explodes the myth of meritocracy and the pretence of improved living standards. While the doom- boomers blame all our ills on trigger happy politicians, Arab oil sheikhs or polluting multinational corporations, the intractable problems of the world have come about through a multiplication of individual attitudes and actions whose end result is industrial anarchy, civil disorders, population explosion and declining standards.

Many of the 'good things' of life- democracy, education, sociology, communications, growth, the welfare state- have contributed to the overall neurosis, trivialization and greed. As these good things will not likely be abandoned, the problems of contemporary society may well be insoluble. But if there are solutions they are unlikely to be implemented because everywhere there is an elitism not of meritocracy but of mediocracy, whose rise can be traced from the 18th century and has accelerated in recent years. No other book relates the discrediting of religion and politics, business and professions so plausibly to chaos in the arts, diminishing returns in education and curbless crime in society. This interdisciplinary book is an interesting read for students of humanities and social sciences.

The Rise of the Mediocracy

David Tribe

Routledge
Taylor & Francis Group

First published in 1975
by George Allen & Unwin Ltd.

This edition first published in 2024 by Routledge
4 Park Square, Milton Park, Abingdon, Oxon, OX14 4RN

and by Routledge
605 Third Avenue, New York, NY 10017

Routledge is an imprint of the Taylor & Francis Group, an informa business

Publisher's Note
The publisher has gone to great lengths to ensure the quality of this reprint but points out that some imperfections in the original copies may be apparent.

Disclaimer
The publisher has made every effort to trace copyright holders and welcomes correspondence from those they have been unable to contact.

A Library of Congress record exists under ISBN: 0043000576

ISBN: 978-1-032-89012-8 (hbk)
ISBN: 978-1-003-54080-9 (ebk)
ISBN: 978-1-032-89014-2 (pbk)

Book DOI 10.4324/9781003540809

The Rise
of the
Mediocracy

by

DAVID TRIBE

London
George Allen & Unwin Ltd
Ruskin House   Museum Street

First published in 1975

ISBN 0 04 300057 6

Printed in Great Britain
in 10pt Times Roman type
by Willmer Brothers Limited
Birkenhead

CONTENTS

Introduction

Curiously we live in perpetual crisis. Rather, we live in perpetual crises. In every newspaper and news bulletin we are confronted by a currency crisis, a liquidity crisis, a food crisis, an energy crisis, an employment crisis, a population crisis, a terrorism crisis, or a thermonuclear crisis – or sometimes all together. In weightier publications we read of less specific crises: a crisis of authority, a crisis of confidence, a moral crisis, a religious crisis.

It is curious for three reasons. The first is a matter of semantics. By definition, a crisis is a moment of decisive change, a turning point. One finds these climaxes, for example, in wars, where certain engagements bring promise of victory, or at least of defeat, peace and reconstruction. Then everyone has something to work for and little time for obsessive-compulsive neuroses or sensational speculations. The crises listed above, however, have none of these characteristics. They do not seem capable of resolution, or at any rate have proceeded for some time without being resolved. Throughout their lingering courses, many people do not have something to work for, or even to hope for, and are devoid of confidence in politics or political leaders, religion or religious leaders, morality or moral leaders (if such can be identified).

These crises are also curious in that they are not overtaking a world engulfed in primordial ignorance. On the contrary, our heads are ringing in the blast of an unprecedented knowledge explosion. This knowledge is not only of the natural world, but, through medicine, psychology and sociology, purports to be knowledge of our society and ourselves.

Most curious of all, the triumph of democracy and education is said to be such that the control of affairs has passed out of the hands of *anciens régimes* and effete ruling classes into those of an élitist meritocracy.

Why, then, is the world in such a mess? Why do we have endemic disruption on a local, national and international level, neurosis, *anomie*, declining standards in all aspects of work and culture, commercialism, hopelessness and trivialisation, or, in the more lurid language of moralists, industrial chaos, civil disorders and world revolution, tension, bloody-mindedness, laziness and incompetence, greed, self-pity and sensationalism? Why is public morale so low that any sort of doom-boom diagnosis is taken literally, and anyone – be he evangelist or ecologist – who foretells the end of the world as confidently as Archbishop Ussher pronounced the start of it is assured of a vast audience and modest fortune?

If we are really in the throes of a terminal illness leading inevitably to nuclear or ecological disaster, identification of presenting signs and symptoms, or even diagnosis, is a purely academic matter. But if, as I believe, the illness is not terminal then diagnosis is important though it may not readily suggest a cure.

Many clinicians of the 'optimistic' school – that is, those who give the world a prognosis outliving this century – suggest we are afflicted with a moral disease, or a social neurosis, where we are in touch with reality and have some insight into our problems but lack the will to solve them. While it is true that our condition may be more psychosomatic than physical, its causation is, save in the broadest context, more than moral and it now has organic manifestations.

The most fashionable 'optimistic' diagnosis is that the world is going through the last throes of a wasting disease, affecting both man and natural resources, brought on by the capitalist virus, but that socialist medicine is starting to bring the patient round. True, there is, in the Western world, new resistance to trigger-happy politicians, Arab oil sheikhs and polluting multinational corporations; but the socialist world, in my view, has regional variations of the underlying pathology. The same may be said of the continued exploitation of the poor by the rich and the weak by the strong.

There is, however, another type of worldwide exploitation which has gone on unnoticed. This is the exploitation of the industrious by the lazy, the provident by the feckless, the childless by the fecund and, above all, the able by the mediocre. Certainly there are, in our society, élite groups that are grasping rich prizes, and it may be that some of them consist, as radical chic maintains, of brilliant meritocrats out of touch with the hopes and fears and limitations of ordinary mortals. The actions of these élitist groups are certainly causing widespread dissatisfaction and a crisis of confidence in traditional institutions. Outside the ranks of trendy lefties, however, this lack of confidence is not so much in the institutions themselves as in the integrity and ability of those running them. Already they are rich in status and substance; let them not also enjoy a spurious reputation for merit and expectation of irremovability.

In a note to my work on 'nucleoethics'[1] I observed that 'the rise of the meritocracy' was 'not to be taken too literally. I propose to write a book on *The Rise of the Mediocracy.'* This announcement did not, I confess, produce a queue of publishers. Social diseases are often deemed unmentionable. Now, however, with the aid of George Allen & Unwin, my silence is broken. Diagnosis will, I suspect, arouse both echoes and protests.

DAVID TRIBE
Sydney 1974

[1] *Nucleoethics: Ethics in Modern Society*, London, 1972, p. 310.

Part One

Theoretical

CHAPTER ONE

Myth of Meritocracy

'Mediocracy has never been more flourishing, able people never more demoralised. . . . Where are the pinnacles of efficiency, craftsmanship, scholarship, creativity, culture and contentment that the forces of human potential might have thrown up?'

In 1958 there appeared an influential book on 'the rise of the meritocracy'.[1] This led to a great vogue of the word 'meritocracy', defined by the author as an 'unpleasant term'[2] of unknown origin. It took its place in popular demonology in a niche of 'cracies' hitherto occupied only by 'bureaucracy'; for 'aristocracy' and 'plutocracy', while not perhaps basking in the radiation of 'democracy', had never been banished to outer darkness.

This was before the golden days of the 'alternative society' which, in the name of equality, preached that parents should be governed by their children, teachers by their pupils, managers by their men, husbands by their wives, psychiatrists by their patients and prison officers by their prisoners. But it was a time when all good socialists and radicals were disturbed by 'élitism', particularly in education. It was not observed that the masses shared this concern. On the contrary, they expected other people, if not themselves, to be specially talented and trained for the jobs they were doing and, at least at that time, were quite content that efficient specialists should receive special status or remuneration. The spearhead of 'egalitarianism' was, in fact, a tiny élite of

[1] Michael Young, *The Rise of the Meritocracy 1870–2033. An essay on education and equality*, London, 1958.
[2] Ibid., p. 153.

affluent intellectuals who did not, on the whole, distribute their fees and royalties to the masses.

The Rise of the Meritocracy was an English fable directed against critics of 'comprehensive education', which was then struggling to bridge the academic gulf between 'grammar' and 'secondary modern' schools set by the 1944 Butler Education Act. This Act establishing universal secondary education decreed that each child should receive schooling appropriate to his or her capacities as determined by an 'eleven-plus' examination at the end of primary education. Those who passed it should go to grammar school, those who failed to secondary modern. There were many practical objections to this system: some children were late developers or chanced to be ill at the time of the exam; while in theory they should be able to transfer to a grammar school at a later age, say thirteen, in practice this was wellnigh impossible; in some areas there were no grammar-school places for all who passed the exam; certain psychologists doubted whether this, or any other single test, could really judge intelligence; many sociologists believed a 'segregated' educational system, whether based on religion, race, sex, class or intellect, was unlikely to produce an integrated community; little thought had been given to what education was suitable for secondary-modern pupils, so they tended to receive an attenuated grammar-school education without the advantages of good morale, specialist teachers or (in 1958) any paper qualification for the great bulk of school leavers. So there developed an irresistible pressure towards common or 'comprehensive' schools. This irresistible force soon ran into immovable objects: refusal of the major religious denominations to abandon their own schools, many of which were also segregated in terms of sex; lack of finance to build new comprehensive schools, save for a handful of show pieces, so that what passed as such were usually merged institutions consisting of buildings scattered inconveniently over a considerable area; teachers' and parents' combined resistance to the closure of the better grammar schools, some of which were ancient and venerable foundations, so that most comprehensive schools did not represent a true cross-section of academic ability.

Envisaging collapse of the move towards comprehensivisation, the 'radical chic' prepared a Counter-Counter-Reformation. It was considerably altruistic of them, since their own children went to neither grammar nor secondary modern schools but to English public (i.e. private) schools which were segregated by every conceivable yardstick. In this campaign *The Rise of the Meritocracy* proved a formidable weapon.

It was a fable, or satire, purportedly written in 2033 by a sociological meritocrat proudly surveying the rise of his class. This could be dated from the 1870s when primary education became compulsory and competitive examinations were introduced to the Civil Service. Whoever constituted the government would be advised by 'not an aristocracy of birth, not a plutocracy of wealth but a true meritocracy of talent'.[1] But it was not until 'education was at last decisively reformed and the family torn away from the feudal embrace'[2] that merit could really come into its own. This began with the 1944 Education Act.

In 1972, the fable ran, Britain began spending more on brilliant than on problem children, and by the 1980s there was rapid social change. Teachers were offered high salaries; meritorious students of all ages, good wages while they studied. Regular intelligence tests were conducted and the higher a student's rating the higher the teacher/student ratio in his class or school. This also determined the subjects he was allowed to study and the type and grade of employment he entered. To allow for late developers and early backsliders, Regional Centres for Adult Education conducted quinquennial reassessments of 'merit' (determined by intelligence and effort), on the basis of which people were promoted or demoted not only in government service but throughout business and industry. The results of National Intelligence Tests were computerised and could be consulted by prospective employers or spouses. Thus 'intelligence' – regarded as 'the ability to raise production, directly or indirectly'[3] – regulated employment, whose stratification and differentials were vastly increased, and marriage. As, subject to some regression towards the mean as described in *The Uses and Abuses of Psychology*,[4] able parents tend to have able children, the meritocracy became an identifiable class.

The working class, renamed 'technicians' and educated in 'modern' schools which taught handicrafts, gymnastics and games and cultivated a Mythos of Muscularity, lost its most able members and potential leaders to the meritocracy. Its political arm, the Technicians' Party (formerly the Labour Party), went

[1] Ibid., p. 19.
[2] Ibid., p. 28.
[3] Ibid., p. 134.
[4] H. J. Eysenck, London, 1953.

into decline and for a time the Conservative Party looked like the party of progress. Following Britain's entry into the Common Market the English meritocracy led the world in inventiveness and productivity. Strikes disappeared after 1991 and massive redundancy caused by automation in industry was overcome by retraining and the formation of a Home Help Corps. This ensured that the meritocrat would not waste time 'trailing around the self-service stores buying the odd packet of potatoes or bucket of frozen fish, cleaning his flat, or cooking the fish, or making his bed' but could instead concentrate on 'the job for which he had been so elaborately trained'.[1] It looked as if the 'battleground between two great principles – the principle of selection by family and the principle of selection by merit'[2] – had finally been occupied by the latter.

By the twenty-first century, however, there were signs of disquiet fomented by women who might once have been called 'blue stockings' and were influenced by sentimental egalitarians from the old Labour Party. In 2009 they captured *The Times* and made it for a while a popular newspaper. This coincided with the issue of a Chelsea Manifesto by a local group of the Technicians' Party. 'Were we', they said, 'to evaluate people, not only according to their intelligence and their education, their occupation and their power, but according to their kindliness and their courage, their imagination and sensitivity, their sympathy and generosity, there could be no classes.'[3] And they were indignant over the great disparity, before 2005, of incomes, and of perks thereafter. Rancour was also building up among certain Conservatives who could not accept that genetic regression in their offspring should lead to 'downward mobility' in employment. Adoption, even kidnapping, of bright children from technicians crept in surreptitiously till regularised by the Welfare of Children Act 2030. These accumulated grievances were magnified by Populists who managed to cause disturbances just before the meritocrat's manuscript was delivered to the publishers, but its author was convinced that such dissidents were 'a hundred years too late. This is the prediction I shall expect to verify when I stand next May listening to the speeches from the great rostrum at Peterloo.'[4] There followed a footnote: 'Since the author of this

1 *The Rise of the Meritocracy*, p. 97.
2 Ibid., p. 24.
3 Ibid., p. 135.
4 Ibid., p. 152.

essay was himself killed at Peterloo, the publishers regret they were not able to submit to him the proofs of his manuscript, for the corrections he might have wished to make before publication. The text, even this last section, has been left exactly as he wrote it. The failings of sociology are as illuminating as its successes.'

They are indeed. Irony directed against a supposititious prophecy of 2033 has turned fiercely against one of 1958. In a Britain prostrate with *malaise anglaise* mediocracy has never been more flourishing, able people never more demoralised – if they have not already emigrated (to receive a doubtful welcome elsewhere). Yet the radical chic continue to inveigh against an imagined meritocracy with a venom which almost makes one suspect that they detect some genetic regression in their offspring, if not in themselves. For the English left-wing Establishment is as hereditary as the right-wing Establishment and differs from it largely in being more exclusive and more waspish.

Yet it is a little surprising that so many people neither radical nor chic should so readily accept the myth of the rise of the meritocracy. In a world otherwise overwhelmed by sociological research this is not the sort of thing likely to be researched; so one falls back on speculation in seeking to explain why the masses should hail a mediocrat as a meritocrat. But what is a mediocrat?

Most of the related words – mediocre, mediocral, mediocriture, mediocrity – were originally used in a neutral or even a laudatory sense. Their Latin origin, akin to Greek, connoted a mountain of middle height, and the words themselves often denoted an Aristotelian mean, or moderation. In periods of religious hysteria or political extremism this was – and is – a quality to be prized.

Pejorative overtones began to sound with the satirical poet Alexander Pope in the eighteenth century: 'A very mediocre poet, one Drayton, is yet taken some notice of, because Selden writ a few notes on one of his poems.'[1] In this pejorative sense 'mediocracy' passed into limited currency: 'The aristocracies must go, the mediocracies which take their place have to fade out.'[2]

[1] Letter to William Warburton, 27 November 1742, in *The Works of Alexander Pope Esq.*, London, 1751, Vol. IX, p. 350.
[2] *Irish Statesman*, cited in *Webster's Third New International Dictionary of the English Language*, Springfield, 1966, p. 1403. 'Mediocrat' appeared in *American Speech*, June 1929, Vol. 4, p. 420. When first proposing to write *The Rise of the Mediocracy* I believed I had coined the word. Only later did I discover the foregoing origins.

Perhaps the first observation to make on 'popular' catchcries for or against 'meritocracy', 'élitism' or 'egalitarianism' is that they are never truly popular. Like 'cultural freedom' and 'utilitarianism' they are the stock-in-trade of middle-class English liberal intellectuals of the nineteenth and twentieth centuries. Through constant repetition in the English-speaking media they have come to assume a wider currency than they actually enjoy among the masses, whose concern is over bread-and-butter issues. This is not an intellectual phenomenon of the English-speaking world alone, and the rise of the mediocracy is a worldwide event, but certain slogans have a peculiarly English connotation. The exhibition of meritocrats – or supposed meritocrats – inveighing against the meritocracy is a symptom of that masochism which, contrary to etymology, has been described as *le vice anglais*.

Equally important to a proper understanding of the mediocracy is the drawing of a distinction between an individual and the class with which he is identified. In an age where writers have been supplanted by sociologists as informed commentators on the social scene, this distinction is archaic, but it remains valid. A 'bureaucrat' may thereby be identified as personally colourful, open and adventurous while the system he serves may be colourless, secretive and cautious. Similarly, a mediocracy represents a congeries of qualities dictated by impersonal social forces and may be served, or even led, by people who are not by nature mediocre.

Indeed, it is probably failure to recognise this basic dichotomy which is chiefly responsible for perpetuation of the myth of meritocracy. For, with the world's population rising dramatically, life expectancy, height, weight and other ponderables among individuals steadily increasing, and accelerating cross-currents amid the globe's genetic pools, it is not unreasonable to posit a rising store of human merit. Channel it through 'equality of opportunity' and the result is – or should be – burgeoning meritocracy. Glance superficially round the world and note the continual breaking of sporting and other physical records, expanding gross national products and growing complexity of technology and government, and it is easy to persuade oneself of the triumph of progress. It is particularly easy if one is a mediocrity and the media one knows are controlled by mediocrats.

Further, if we take the first few decades of the period surveyed in *The Rise of the Meritocracy*, viz. 1870–1910, and extend it back through the nineteenth century, we can see good reason for the 'cult of progress' that then emerged and has never been submerged. For the eighteenth century liberated forces of both progress and regress, whose strengths and confronting inertias were different and whose resolution only history could demonstrate. Throughout the nineteenth century progress was dominant. There were areas like architecture and town planning where mediocracy established an early foothold, but in such diverse fields as political and social justice, education, science, communications, health and welfare, advances were surely made. And in some of them, e.g. air transport, weaponry and life-saving drugs, advances have continued. Yet even here side-effects, or in the case of weaponry direct effects, have progressed even faster, so that it is by no means demonstrable that mankind is 'better off' for these developments. And when today we survey the whole landscape of human endeavour, where are the pinnacles of efficiency, craftsmanship, scholarship, creativity, culture and contentment that the forces of human potential might have thrown up? Or if, by another trendy metaphor, man is in the saddle directing the course of psycho-social evolution, in what direction is he galloping?

CHAPTER TWO

Rise of Democracy

'The democratic process involves levelling down as well as up. . . .
In many important particulars levelling down is more conspicuous.
. . . The whole of society, socialist and non-socialist, is emasculated
by Marxist sloganeering.'

One of the most pervasive of modern myths is that of a golden age buried in the distant sands of time. Since the sands were prehistoric this theory has the philosophical disadvantage and practical advantage of being non-falsifiable by historical dredging. It owes much to the Rousseauan concept of the 'noble savage' before he was corrupted by government and the Marxist hypothesis of 'primitive communism', though it is supported by sentimental egalitarians who are not Marxists and have never heard of Rousseau. Anthropological researches of the nineteenth and twentieth centuries into 'primitive' communities have failed to establish an idyllic setting of simplicity, tranquillity and equality. On the contrary, such communities show considerable political and social complexity and stratification, a flourishing 'pecking order' and a patriarchal leadership of sanctified witch-doctors and imperious elders. While certain tribal land and amenities are held 'in common', individual status tends to be indicated not only by size of domicile, number of utensils, wealth of ornamentation and lethalness of weapons, but by number of wives. Though there may be meeting-houses to discuss matters of common interest, women are rarely allowed to speak and children never. Yet this is the sort of society lauded by today's 'underground' press.

Whatever may have obtained in prehistoric times, early history shows the existence, five thousand or more years ago, of Egyptian, Sumerian and Indo-European empires, which established a pattern unbroken till the rise of Periclean Athens. Since its brief moment of glory it has been lauded by all radical-chic writers as the 'cradle of democracy'. And for affluent, male, Greek, conformist intellectuals it was indeed attractive. The fact that it was sustained by slavery, paternalistic, racist and given to banishing heretics is a circumstance overlooked – or never known – by the fashionable progressives that do it honour. Of course it was a haven of civilisation and culture, but this is another question entirely.

After the glory that was Greece came the grandeur that was Rome, glumness that was Christianity and grimness that was feudalism, and democracy ceased to be even a theoretical ideal. After long centuries it began to emerge in modern guise. Generally this is dated to ideas that flourished in many places and events that occurred in France and the United States in the eighteenth century. Certainly from these can be dated the rise of the mediocracy. The radical scenario of the emergence of democracy on its upward climb to 'people's democracy' is now, however, dated to elements that briefly surfaced among Anabaptists in the sixteenth century or during the seventeenth-century English Civil War, till they were beaten into the ground by orthodox Reformers or by Cromwell. Thereafter true lineal descent is disputed. Without trying to differentiate between Marxists and non-Marxists or one expert and another, we may simply draw up, in chronological order, the following documents: a 'remonstrance' by English Levellers (1649); a 'declaration' by their yet more radical offshoot, the English Diggers (1649); the American 'declaration of independence' (1776); the French Revolutionary 'declaration of the rights of man and of citizens' (1789); the 'communist manifesto' of Marx and Engels (1848).

Interestingly, perusal of these classics does not show, with the exception of the American affirmation that 'all men are created equal', much encouragement to a mediocracy. Rather, they were concerned to overthrow the tyranny of caste and hereditary privilege, of unjust laws and corrupt administration, of commercial and colonial exploitation. The enemy was enslavement, not élitism; expropriation, not excellence.

From the Levellers came protest against 'the present transac-

tion of affaires', which was 'both arbytrary and tyrannicall',[1]
and call for free elections and honest government: eminently
reasonable proposals. Apart from expressing a 'desire to manure,
dig, and plant in the waste grounds and Commons' – from which
object their name was derived – the 'red revolutionary' Diggers
protested 'against all Arbitrary Courts, Terms, Lawyers, Impro-
priators, Lords of Mannors, Patents, Priviledges, Customs, Tolls,
Monopolisers, Incroachers, Inhancers, etc., or any other interest-
parties, whose powers are Arbitrary',[2] denounced tithes and
military courts in peacetime, and wished to replace the Norman
with the Anglo-Saxon feudal system. Having asserted that all men
are created equal, the American *Declaration of Independence*
went on to give a less than egalitarian exposition: 'that they are
endowed by their creator with certain unalienable rights; – that
among these are life, liberty, and the pursuit of happiness; – that
to secure these rights, governments are instituted among men,
deriving their just powers from the consent of the governed'.[3]
The French Revolutionaries declared that public ills and the
corruption of governments were attributable solely to ignoring,
forgetting or scorning 'natural rights, inalienable and sacred to
man'.[4] In their denunciation of the bourgeoisie Marx and Engels
looked nostalgically back to 'feudal, patriarchal, idyllic
relations', the 'motley feudal ties that bound man to his "natural
superiors" ' and 'the most heavenly ecstasies of religious fervour,
of chivalrous enthusiasm, of philanthropic sentimentalism'.[5]

   The authors of these documents were not, perhaps, to blame
for the élitism that succeeded them, though it was a little
unfortunate that the Levellers and the Diggers were so quickly
followed by Lord Protector Cromwell, the American Revolutionaries by a community divided by sociologists into nine social
classes (where Britain has five), and the French Revolutionaries
by Emperor Napoleon. Marx and Engels wanted 'dictatorship of

[1] Anon., *The Levellers Remonstrance*, London, 10 May 1649, p. 2.
[2] Gerrard Winstanley, *A Declaration of the Wel-affected in the County of Buckinghamshire*, London, 1649, pp. 8 and 7.
[3] *The Constitutions of the United States, according to the Latest Amendments; to which are annexed, the Declaration of Independence; and the Federal Constitution; with the Amendments Thereto*, Philadelphia, 1791, p. 158.
[4] *La Déclaration des Droits de l'Homme et des Citoyens*, Paris, 20–26 August 1789.
[5] *Manifesto of the Communist Party*, London, 1848, by Karl Marx and Friedrich Engels: ed. by Engels, 1888, p. 9.

the proletariat' mediated by a Communist Party but did not live to see 'the new class'[1] of privileged *apparatchiki*.

When we turn to the writings and communities associated with 'utopian socialists' and 'utopian communists' like Robert Owen, and with sundry hippies and religious fundamentalists in our day, we see that 'popular' movements – as distinct from 'popular' historians – have never been averse to élitism so long as it flies the right political colours. And this is not a mere intellectual élitism forced on conspirators in an alien society but an élitism that manifests in practical authoritarianism when left to its own devices. For Owen deemed it 'self-evident' that 'any character, from the best to the worst, from the most ignorant to the most enlightened, may be given to any community, even to the world at large, by applying certain means; which are to a great extent at the command and under the controul, or easily made so, of those who possess the Government of Nations'.[2]

Clearly, the chief message of prophets of modern left-wing politics was directed not to a mediocracy but to a meritocracy of able, dedicated, socially conscious reformers or revolutionaries, who might come from any social class. In fact, most of them came from the middle classes, while in France a substantial proportion were aristocrats. Whatever their individual philosophies, they wished to provide opportunities for village Hampdens and mute, inglorious Miltons who had languished in backwaters of feudal Europe and colonial America. They believed in free enquiry, convinced that their ideas would gain by comparison with opposing views, in initiative and hard work. Beyond new frontiers they saw visions of great societies, and they were, for the most part, anxious to advance the technocrats' revolution in the interests of all. Sometimes they worked with 'bourgeois' reformers in the tradition of *laissez-faire* capitalism, who stimulated the cult of progress with cults of individualism, self-reliance and self-help. Throughout the nineteenth century, they promoted meritocrats in politics, trades unions, universities, professions and business, the media and powerful voluntary

1 Milovan Djilas, *The New Class. An Analysis of the Communist System*, London, 1957.
2 Robert Owen, *A New View of Society: or, Essays on the Principle of the Formation of the Human Character, and the Application of the Principle to Practice*, London, 1813, p. 9.

societies. Together they fragmented the cracking feudal system and injected the more able and energetic members of the middle classes into the upper and of the lower into the middle.

Social mobility was, however, only one element in the pre-conditions for nineteenth-century prosperity. It was, after all, a process which was not begun, simply speeded up. Even in the Middle Ages able people could rise in social class, if only through entering the Church; and if, from the sixteenth century, royal favours were not open to all social classes, they reached well down into the *petit bourgeoisie*. Many other forces were at work in the nineteenth century than social mobility. Some of them were more important. Public accountability – another product of the democratic movement – reduced corruption and raised efficiency in government. Free enquiry undermined the ideological and then the political foundation of the Church as a vested interest able to retard the scientific and technological revolution. Improved European technology opened up the world to Western imperialism, comprehensive sources of raw materials and new markets. Apart from sporadic skirmishes in Europe and America and constant skirmishing on the borders of empire, there was no major, debilitating international war between the Napoleonic Wars and the First World War a century later.

As these favourable impulses ran out of steam, or were actually reversed, in the twentieth century, other forces un-leashed by democracy became more apparent. They should not have taken anyone by surprise, for shrewd commentators had detected them at all stages of the democratic progress. But the mediocracy was by then well entrenched, and mediocracies are always taken by surprise.

In 1748 one of France's leading political theorists – and him-self an aristocrat – Montesquieu, adumbrated the social situation in a republic:

> Since every individual ought here to enjoy the same happiness and the same advantages, they should consequently taste the same pleasures and form the same hopes, which cannot be expected but from a general frugality.... The good sense and happiness of individuals depend greatly on the mediocrity of their abilities and fortunes. Therefore, as a republic, where the laws have placed many in a middling station, is composed of

wise men, it will be wisely governed; as it is composed of happy men, it will be extremely happy.'[1]

He added that 'when a democracy is founded in commerce, private people may acquire vast riches without a corruption of morals' for 'every wealthy citizen in such a mediocrity' is 'obliged to take some pains either in preserving or acquiring a fortune'[2]. But he sometimes spoke of 'mediocrity' in the sense of 'mediocracy'. It is an interesting, if controversial, assertion – which partly foreshadows Freud – that people are sensible and happy when their abilities and fortunes are mediocre. It is clearly behind the American founding fathers' concatenation of equality, life, liberty and the pursuit of happiness; and in the light of subsequent history, must be deemed at least arguable. What makes it further interesting is that it is an early acknowledgement from a seminal author that the democratic process involves levelling down as well as up. This contrasts with the sanguine conviction of nineteenth- and twentieth-century advanced writers that one need anticipate only levelling up. My contention is that, while in some material matters (energy consumption) everyone is being levelled up, at least in the developed world, and in others (guaranteed income) there is levelling both up and down, in many important particulars levelling down is more conspicuous. These particulars will feature in later chapters.

When liberal intellectuals of the Enlightenment spoke of *liberté, égalité, fraternité,* they were not thinking of mob rule. Liberty was not licence; equality meant equality before the law, and perhaps equality of opportunity and equal franchise, not ciphered equality; fraternity did not mean that every musical *salon* and literary *soirée* in private homes was open to passing revellers. Unfortunately, the French Revolution – a great turning point in human history – went far beyond the righting of wrongs that most radicals had envisaged. An early detector of danger was Edmund Burke.

'The effect of liberty to individuals is', he declared, 'that they may do what they please: We ought to see what it will please them to do, before we risque congratulations, which may be soon turned into complaints. . . . Who could flatter himself that

[1] Charles de Secondat, Baron de Montesquieu, *De L'esprit des loix* [*lois*], Paris, 1748, tr. by Thomas Nugent as *The Spirit of Laws*, London, 1823, Vol. I, p. 40.
[2] Ibid., pp. 44–5.

those men, suddenly, and, as it were, by enchantment, snatched from the humblest rank of subordination, would not be intoxicated with their unprepared greatness? ... Along with its natural protectors and guardians, learning will be cast into the mire, and trodden down under the hoofs of a swinish multitude.'[1]

Although he denied that blood, names and titles, instead of 'virtue and wisdom, actual or presumptive,' were qualifications for government, and declared that anything limiting the 'rights of men' was 'so much of fraud and injustice',[2] Burke has entered history undeservedly branded as a reactionary. It was his misfortune to have phrases like 'swinish multitude' quoted out of context and to have provoked the brilliant reformer Thomas Paine to write *Rights of Man*. But while Paine demolished monarchy and the mystical notion of 'property' and has inspired generations of fighters against tyranny round the world, he did not really answer Burke's attack on unregulated liberty, equality and fraternity. With the sacrifice of Lavoisier to mob passions in 1794 the power of fanatical hoofs was amply demonstrated, and it is somewhat ironic that Paine himself would have gone the same way but for a gaoler's blunder.

Though radicals continued to denounce Burke, some of them remembered the lessons of the French Revolution. In his classic essay *On Liberty* Mill observed that 'in political speculations "the tyranny of the majority" is now generally included among the evils against which society requires to be on its guard',[3] though this caution tended to undermine his own concept of utilitarianism. Usually defined as advocating government to ensure the 'greatest happiness of the greatest number', this concept overlooks the fact that persecuting minorities is probably that pastime which gives the majority both its greatest happiness and its greatest sense of self-righteousness. At all events, when the issue of universal suffrage, to which he had at first committed himself, became a major talking-point in the 1860s, Mill sought to modify it by giving more than one vote to the wealthier classes. Another radical, George Jacob Holyoake, proposed an 'Intelligence Franchise' since 'he is not a democrat, but an

---

1 *Reflections on the Revolution in France, and on the Proceedings in London relative to that Event*, London, 1790, pp. 9, 62 and 117.
2 Ibid., pp. 73, 74 and 86.
3 *On Liberty*, London, 1859, p. 13.

anarchist, who insists that the vote of the most ignorant shall count for as much as that of the most highly educated class in the community'.[1]

In the popular firmament a power struggle between anarchists and communists dominated the second half of the nineteenth century and part of the twentieth. It might almost be called a class struggle, since the anarchist leaders were aristocratic and the communist bourgeois; it was certainly a personality clash. Marx and Engels thought the conflict of paramount ideological importance, though a leading Russian *émigré* thought the two philosophies compatible: 'We shall build on new foundations – those of Communism and Anarchy and not those of Individualism and Authority.'[2] What they had in common were leaders whose own backgrounds induced an optimistic belief in the disinterest, self-discipline and ability of the population as a whole. Not surprisingly, neither philosophy has been implemented or seems likely to be.

But if academic communism or anarchism is a distant dream, certain vulgarisations are neither distant nor immaterial. In stressing the 'dignity of labour', which Marx intended to include mental labour, Marxists have glorified manual labour regardless of its productivity. At the same time, concentration on the means of production, distribution and exchange has elevated the creation of consumer products into a cult rather than a prelude to the good life. Things have become more important, as well as less embarrassing, than new ideas. Moreover, by relating this production of things to a dictatorship of the 'proletariat', Marxists have devalued those qualities which, in a technological age, are of prime importance: inventiveness, initiative and management skills. The ablest of Marxist leaders are, of course, well aware of a need for these qualities – and are ready to import them from capitalist or fascist nations – but the whole of society, socialist and non-socialist, is emasculated by Marxist sloganeering. Not for the first time have slogans obscured what they sought to clarify and turned mediocrities into messiahs. After a lifetime of trendy leftism and singing lullabies to the cradle of socialism, George Bernard Shaw belatedly came to recognise: 'This haphazard Mobocracy must be replaced by democratic aristocracy: that is, by the dictatorship, not of the whole proletariat, but

---

[1] *The Liberal Situation: Necessity for A Qualified Franchise*, London, 1865, pp. 9–10.
[2] Prince Peter Kropotkin, *Le Salariat*, London, 1889, p. 34.

of that five per cent of it capable of conceiving the job and pioneering in the drive towards its divine goal.'[1] Similar distinction may be made between academic and practical anarchism. Can sophisticated exponents of the destruction of government really be surprised when certain of their disciples reach for a bomb?

[1] *Fabian Essays*, London, 1948 ed, Postscript, 'Sixty Years of Fabianism', p. 223.

CHAPTER THREE

Hereditary Privilegentsias

'What the rise of democracy has achieved is not the abolition of privilege, but a proliferation of hereditary privilegentsias into all walks of life.... Social mobility is one of the great myths of our time.'

The early radicals followed Jean Meslier, whose 'testament'[1] was published posthumously by Voltaire, in their dual opposition to the Monarchy and the Church. As it was picturesquely put, social justice would come only when the last king had been strangled by the entrails of the last priest. Why should government be vested in the genetic lottery of a particular family, which could throw up mongols or monsters as readily as scholars or saints? 'The idea of hereditary legislators', said Thomas Paine, 'is as inconsistent as that of hereditary judges, or hereditary juries; and as absurd as an hereditary mathematician, or an hereditary wise man; and as ridiculous as an hereditary poet-laureate.'[2] In effect, an hereditary monarchy was usually linchpin of a system which did include something like hereditary judges and juries, if not hereditary mathematicians, wise men and poets-laureate. Round the Court there grew up those 'ridiculous sinecures' which Sir Charles Dilke believed did 'much towards continuing the political demoralisation in high places which all of us deplore'.[3] Adding a holy gilt to the lily was a

[1] *Mon Testament*, Geneva, 1762.
[2] *Rights of Man: Being an Answer to Mr Burke's Attack on the French Revolution*, London, 1791–2, Part I, p. 71.
[3] *The Cost of the Crown*, London, 1871, pp 7–9.

priesthood which was in theory open to all social classes, but which became increasingly dominated by the social class which controlled the secular administration, and especially by its duller and drabber members. Until the eighteenth century, baronial wars, wars of succession and religious wars at least weeded out the least efficient popes and princes. Thereafter, as the upper classes coalesced in opposition to popular revolutions, an hereditary oligarchy tended to become an hereditary mediocracy.

Virtually all the early radicals hoped eventually to abolish classes or castes according to their several philosophies. The utopian anarchists and communists believed this would come about through the abolition of private property or ownership of productive potential. The 'bourgeois' radicals, who came from all social classes, wished simply to maximise social mobility. In effect, like some moderate socialists, they believed in meritocracy. They did not see this as the creation of a new class, though Bernard Shaw called it a 'Democratic Aristocracy'. His concern was that, under the existing class structure, 'sexual selection, which is still the masterkey to eugenics in a healthy population, is most mischievously restricted'[1] by socio-economic bars to marriage. He did not enquire whether professors would be more likely to marry the clever daughters of sewerage workers under Democratic Aristocracy than dukes to marry chorus girls under the old order.

Towards the end of the nineteenth century, however, Marxists and 'fellow travellers' – who deserve their anaemic label as much for their lack of Marxist scholarship and their ignorance of world events as for their moral turpitude – began their climb to ascendancy in non-conservative politics. And from that point popular rage was diverted from the aristocracy to the bourgeoisie.

When Engels had, like Owen before him and a blessed band of socialist millionaires after him, safely amassed his fortune, he and Marx discovered that capitalism

> has left remaining no other nexus between man and man than naked self-interest, than callous 'cash payment'. . . . It has resolved personal worth into exchange value, and in place of the numberless indefeasible chartered freedoms, has set up that single, unconscionable freedom – Free Trade. In one word, for

[1] 'Postscript' to 1948 ed. of *Fabian Essays*, p. 218.

exploitation, veiled by religious and political illusions, it has substituted naked, shameless, direct, brutal exploitation.[1]

It would appear that the main complaint against capitalists was that they exploited openly and unaided while landowners did it under the decent guise of religion. Fortified by innumerable tactical arguments and party lines, this attitude ensured that before the upper-class hegemony or social influence of the churches had been properly eroded, all socialist attention was turned to the 'class struggle' between the proletariat and the bourgeoisie. In popular demonology the multinational corporation took the place of the multinational Vatican, and industrialists were slated for paying too little tax while monarchs, churches and property speculators paid no tax at all.

This process was latterly aided by a systematic onslaught by media mediocrats against the nineteenth century. Of course the century provided objectionable targets: human exploitation and urban ugliness during rapid industrialisation (though scarcely to the same extent as in some socialist countries in the twentieth century), bourgeois artistic tastelessness (though scarcely to the same extent as proletarian artistic tastelessness in an age of supermarket knick-knackery and do-it-yourself) and moralistic self-righteousness and puritanism (though scarcely to the same extent as in some socialist countries in the twentieth century). That opposition to the nineteenth century was not motivated chiefly by cultural libertarianism was shown when media mediocrats were joined by prattling parsons. In contemning and condemning an age described as egocentric, materialistic, unsophisticated and – worst sin of all – old-fashioned, they forgot to explain how a band of itinerant hot-gospellers in a peasant backwater of a corrupt first-century empire could be regarded as 'modern' and 'relevant'.

The truth is that these 'old-fashioned' nineteenth-century rationalists, individualists and liberal reformers were well aware of their century's shortcomings. By the end of it they had got women and children out of mines and factories into their own homes and into schools. It has taken the twentieth century to reinstate the 'working wife' and find a new source of wealth in children – in television commercials instead of up chimneys. What has motivated the attack on the nineteenth century is recognition that it provided the most fundamental attack on

---

[1] *Communist Manifesto*, 1888 ed., p. 9.

B

vested interests in church and state – and on mediocracy.

Today, Victorian reformers are remembered for their atheism or their republicanism, which our mediocrats are pleased to call 'dead horses'. In a world context they are far from dead, and where they have died the mediocrats have massacred them. But the liberals of last century were far from fixated on these questions, important as they are. Throughout the nineteenth century attention was directed to birth control, which will be considered later, and land law reform. This was concerned with such issues as abolition of the game laws, which put aristocratic sport before peasant sustenance, abolition of the English laws of primogeniture and entail, which kept a lot of land permanently off the market to create endemic scarcity, reduction of legal expenses during land transfers and provision of greater security of tenure to cultivators who effected improvements. As the nineteenth-century secularist Charles Bradlaugh pointed out:

> In a country like our own the ownership of property has surely its duties as well as its rights. The labourer able to work who will not work is prosecuted and punished as a rogue and a vagabond.... Unoccupied and unused land near great towns escapes the local rating, whilst its value for building purposes is often enormously increased by the mere augmentation of population. Why should the owner of this land escape its proper burden any more than the labourer, who is punished if he tries to escape?[1]

And some nineteenth-century reformers who were not in favour of the public ownership of the means of production, distribution and exchange, on the grounds that this would diminish incentive and productivity, were in favour of land nationalisation.

In terms of the Marxist analysis, however, landowners merely collected a modest rent from capitalists who made a monstrous profit from the 'surplus value' of labour, and the only aristocrats to be denounced were those shrewdies who put their resources into early developmental projects like mines, canals, bridges and railways. As late as 1958 many socialists believed that 'wealth in land had ceased to count'[2] and looked with benevolent sympathy on those upper-class mediocrities who had eschewed capitalist entrepreneurship, with all its nasty connotations of

[1] *Compulsory Cultivation of Land: What it Means, and Why it Ought to be Enforced*, London, 1887, p. 5.
[2] *The Rise of the Meritocracy*, p. 153.

'trade', in favour of sitting tight on their decaying estates. Today it is surely clear to all that the great unearned fortunes of our time have been made by those who inherited or purchased at the right time land 'near great towns', above natural resources, or almost anywhere; and that in times of inflation those things which have inflated most are not manufactured goods, which may even have become cheaper, but food, rent or mortgages. As populations explode it is land ownership which gives risk-free fortunes to mediocracies, hereditary or *parvenu*. Yet, characteristically, not a word of acknowledgement to the nineteenth-century meritocrats who foresaw this outcome has come from the trendy mediocrats who flourish in our own sophisticated age. Prematurely lamenting exhaustion of practically every natural resource through the machinations of multinational corporations, they seem oblivious of the one identifiable resource that is non-expansible: land. Or, if the problem is acknowledged, they speak airily of colonisation of distant planets or other solar systems.

In its heyday republican literature was directed less against the aristocracy at large than against its pinnacle, the monarchy, especially the French, English and Russian royal families. Though this literature insisted the case against monarchy was impersonal, both it and popular movements that surrounded it flourished when royal incumbents were personally unpopular. Since the aristocratic system functioned on the principle of *noblesse oblige* – and not simply on devotion to some mechanistic principle of inheritance – monarchs were less unpopular when they were imperious than when they were lazy or inefficient. As a group the upper classes were widely expected to diffuse culture, learning, good taste and morality through society at large. Whether queen bees were adored or abandoned depended on their provision of royal jelly.

Before the twentieth century, aristocratic families, royal and non-royal, were fairly productive of men and women of genius, especially in literature and learning. For reasons that have not been properly investigated, such productivity is now in decline. One might say that with the death of Bertrand Russell has come the *Götterdämmerung* of aristocratic culture. As it is also believed that the power of aristocracy has collapsed, their cultural twilight might be consistent with a general rise of the meritocracy. But has their power collapsed?

Outside some countries of the Third World, where absolutism

still prevails, hereditary rulers wield a shadow of their former power. They face, however, but a shadow of their former hazards. In primitive communities they might once have been offered up to the gods as living sacrifices, noblest and most acceptable; till the eighteenth century they were expected to lead their forces into battle personally, if not engage in single combat to resolve a feud, vicariously sustained and vicariously suspended. Should they be deposed they were likely to face death or penurious exile. Now that ex-potentates live comfortably in Mediterranean watering-places on secret banking accounts and reigning grandees live longer and sleep more soundly, it is not to be wondered at that their powers have become more ceremonial than actual. Outside reigning families hereditary aristocracies retain legislative functions in a dwindling number of countries. Yet this need not unduly concern them as political power tends to shift from the legislature to the executive, from the executive to the bureaucracy, and from the bureaucracy to international financiers. This is where the political situation is 'normal'. In a growing number of lands the situation is 'abnormal' and the colonels have taken over. Whatever style of government prevails, there tends today to be a collapse of authority in real terms and in all spheres of life, so that even an archbishop cannot rely on unquestioning obedience from his own domestic chaplain. In this sense hereditary oligarchies have been downgraded – like everybody else.

Outside the naked exercise of power, however, there is little evidence of aristocratic eclipse. Certainly the impotent or the improvident have vanished, but any good reference book on the peerage shows this has always been so. Certainly they have fewer servants than of yore, but the servant class (despite wild foreshadowing of a Home Help Corps in *The Rise of the Meritocracy*) is a dying class and the aristocracy has managed to keep a notable proportion of survivors. For not only have the upper classes retained high *per capita* purchasing power but they are still assumed by gentlemen's gentlemen to be productive of gentlemen. Their capacity to retain wealth in supposedly democratic – not to say 'meritocratic' – societies is both a cause and a result of their continuing influence: something which trendy sociologists have, on the whole, overlooked.

At the seedier level it is as true today as during the triumphal lifetime of the mythical Duke of Plaza-Toro,

In short, if you'd kindle
The spark of a swindle,
Lure simpletons into your clutches –
Yes; into your clutches –
Or hoodwink a debtor,
You cannot do better
Than trot out a duke or a duchess.[1]

In the world of genuine finance and industry, company directorships and consultancies of a non-onerous kind are readily available to any aristocrat able to sign prospectuses or reports with a
minimum of blots (greatly facilitated by ballpoint pens), while
noblemen with a modicum of business ability are prominent
among international merchant bankers and on the boards of
finance houses whose decisions help freeze or free credit, halt or
generate employment, trigger inflation or recession, initiate runs
on currency and topple financially discredited governments
round the world. This, perhaps the least publicised of aristocratic
activities, is unquestionably the most important and, in some
respects, dwarfs legislative powers of yesteryear. More publicised
activities are of less concern to the general public but significant
in special fields. Largely through banal biographies of dead
monarchs or intimate accounts of living ones, noble authors have
a continuing, perhaps a growing, hold on supposedly serious
literature in their own right, while *protégés* in the arts have
thriven on noble influence as voluptuously in the twentieth
century as in the eighteenth when their patrons were universally
acknowledged arbiters of taste. And one might pass from the
trendy arts to the crafts, to international fashion and design, to
the chic cultivation of leisure – in short, to anything where there
are no objective standards of excellence but a combination of
personal whim and deference to *la mode* – noting how the royal
road to success is richly signposted with noble names. In all fields
of life along the road one can see people taking sustenance for
the journey from private schools and private clubs, private bene-
factions and private trusts – with noble coats of arms on many
wrought-iron entrance gates. Hardly surprising, therefore, that
glossy magazines and popular tabloids should, to the consternation and incomprehension of Marxist mediocrats, accept the

[1] W. S. Gilbert, *The Gondoliers; or The King of Barataria*, London, 1889,
Act II.

situation and luxuriate in royal romances and lovey-dovey lord-
lings, indigenous or foreign.

Marxism is against parasitism, and in some socialist countries
has set landowners to work on their expropriated estates. But it
has tended to be more concerned about the proletariat than
about the peasantry and has had simplistic notions on how
economic changes, chiefly at the factory level, will change
political, social and psychological realities. Consciously or un-
consciously it has largely, on coming to power, taken over the
attitudes and apparatus of the ancient ruling classes, i.e. traditional hereditary oligarchies who regarded 'alien' *parvenu*
industrialists as hostilely as do the Marxists themselves. Thus
'communist' revolutions have tended to lead to 'national socialism', with primitive power structures intact, rather than egalitarian international socialism. In the very many countries where
such revolutions have not taken place Marxism has merely
diverted popular indignation from the inequity of incomes and
assets and the iniquity of hereditary privileges derived from land,
towards the 'real enemy' – the capitalist class. Nineteenth-
century radical reformism, which sought to abolish traditional
class barriers and benefits, has been replaced by an urban
charade of unresolved 'class struggle'.

As a result, the aristocracy has an affluence and influence (if
only derived from tourism) in the twentieth century that it could
hardly have ventured to hope for in the nineteenth. What the rise
of democracy has achieved is not the abolition of privilege, but a
proliferation of hereditary privilegentsias into all walks of life.
Instead of dissolving, classes have largely turned into castes.
Thomas Paine's irony has recoiled. Hereditary legislators have
ceased to look inconsistent, absurd or ridiculous since they were
joined by hereditary judges, jurors, mathematicians, wise men
and poets-laureate (or television personalities). In some countries
this happy result has been achieved with the help of education. In
Paine's England (and France and the United States) the children
of the ruling classes were taught by anonymous tutors. By the
nineteenth and twentieth centuries they went to anything but
anonymous public (i.e. private) schools. The meritocratic fore-
cast of 1958, to the effect that the better ones would be absorbed
by the State and the others would be impoverished and downgraded, has proved as reliable as other forecasts of this genre. It
could at least claim boldness, since a report issued in the same

year showed that the English 'establishment'[1] was enriched by public schoolmen to the extent of most officers of the armed forces, all but one High Court Justice, all but one Anglican Bishop, all the then Conservative Cabinet, almost all Conservative Members of Parliament and – most significant of all – one-third of Labour Members of Parliament. If the figures are slightly less impressive today, the explanation is more likely to be in terms of the declining power of learning and traditional institutions than of any diminution in hereditary privilege.

Largely because of their charitable status and their property endowments English public schools are richer and more prestigious than ever, while so great is the pressure to get into them and so hereditary the flood-gates that many will accept, at birth, only the sons of former pupils. The lucky entrants may also be the grandsons of former pupils, whose financing of their education has the added benefit of reducing taxation or death duties. Dr Thomas Arnold would be truly astonished to see what a haven of nepotism and tax avoidance his halls of self-reliance have become.

Throughout the world a lot more self-reliance has vanished since Dr Arnold's nineteenth century. The great industrial empires carved out by barons of industry have become as hereditary as most other empires. So have the great financial empires. Liberal intellectuality might not dispassionately be thought of as an hereditary quality, and neither liberalism nor intellectualism is flourishing, but liberal intellectual dynasties command most heights in what passes for letters or learning.

The hereditary system knows no political or class barriers. Left-wing establishments are as numerous and self-perpetuating as right-wing establishments. The poorest tied cottage or subsidised flat is passed on to offspring as jealously as the grandest castle. Sons of miners and dockers inherit their fathers' union tickets more surely than sons of doctors and lawyers inherit their fathers' practices. Social mobility is one of the great myths of our time.

Divers hereditary privilegentsias, each with its powers and perks, however puny, have diverse social consequences. Who can complain or effectively campaign against corruption in high places when there is such manifest corruption in low places? And

[1] John Vaizey, 'The Public School', in *The Establishment. A Symposium* ed. by Hugh Thomas, London, 1959.

wherever corruption flourishes, mediocrity abounds. So too does social injustice. Having no theory of 'divine right' or popular consensus behind or beneath them, and no ability within them, these new privilegentsias survive by nothing but solidarity and self-seeking. Even more than the older privilegentsias they must oppose the advancement of women, racial minorities or other traditionally unprivileged groups; for if civil-rights legislation were to open up their enclaves to members of these groups on ideological grounds, they would be vulnerable to outsiders on any grounds – even the grounds of merit. And so we weep as journalistic mediocracies call for social justice in the name of the working classes, while the working classes plot and scheme to deny it to lesser brethren.

CHAPTER FOUR

Collapse of Systems

'Now that the universe as a whole does not "make sense", trendy experimenters are under no obligation to "make sense" of any of their "findings". . . . As "expediency", "experimentation" and "innovation" take the place of systems in politics, science and the arts, no mediocrat need fear unemployment.'

However irksome the feudal system may have been to men of towering genius, whose brows were seldom exposed even to the laurel wreaths of history, it gave to the generality of mankind a sense of place and purpose. Most medieval men had a ceiling to ambition and a floor to adversity. They lived in a nexus of established rights and established duties decreed by a universal moral law. Understanding and interpreting this law was part of the function of theology, which was widely recognised as the queen of the sciences. In this way a political system sustained a social system and was itself sustained by an intellectual system.

That the intellectual system was false and the social and political systems unstable are facts of history. That life within them was not as idyllic as Pre-Raphaelite or Marxist legend might suggest is matter for debate. To what extent their collapse has assisted the rise of the mediocracy is the only issue that concerns us here. The effect on such abstractions as happiness or human dignity is far too subtle to qualify for meaningful debate.

The older hereditary privilegentsias were recognised not only by 'birth', which signalised the lower classes as much as the upper, or by 'breeding', which was not always a conspicuous cultural success, but by public responsibilities. In the eyes of their contemporaries they were, in the last analysis, judged on whether these responsibilities (providing employment, winning wars, building castles and churches, organising the local 'welfare state') were well or badly carried out. They usually had to be courageous, but it hardly mattered whether they were personally clever or comely as they monopolised superficial aids to brilliance or beauty and were both publicly and privately eulogised whatever their actual attainments. As long as the political climate, internal and external, was moderately serene, their social position was assured. They could therefore afford to employ as advisers, confidants and executive officers in the many functions for which they were responsible, the ablest people available. Looking back today we may have reservations about the conceptual framework of their society, but we can have little cause to criticise the artistry and craftsmanship that gave to this framework an enduring structure.

When a system like the feudal system collapses one expects to find a meritocracy undermining the foundation, which was too rigid, too immobile, too open to corruption, too closed to new ideas. The arguments for change are many and obvious. Able people should be more than executants, but untrammelled creators, planners, ordainers. And when one reviews the all-round men of genius who flourished in the Renaissance and – limited somewhat by specialisation as knowledge grew – the Enlightenment, it does indeed seem that an aristocracy has been overshadowed by a meritocracy, even if sociologists might identify both as from the same socio-economic class. And, of course, an élite based on talent feels itself as unchallenged as one based on 'divine right'. Only a mediocracy, which sees on every side a grand perspective of other 'average men' who could fill its shoes with comparable distinction, which rests on no ideological foundation other than a populist interpretation of 'democracy', sees its authority as under constant challenge. Only a mediocracy consists of rulers and opinion-formers who surround themselves with people more mediocre than themselves and thereby allay suspicion of neighbourly ambition or ability. Of all political 'systems' only a mediocracy is likely to strangle itself through constantly looking over its shoulder.

Any leadership may sink into a gerontocracy whose ageing and failing rulers are jealous of the young and dynamic. Though they teach others to venerate age for its own sake, they do not worship it themselves. In the same way, mediocracy which need only glory in its mediocrity seems peculiarly jealous of merit. In

reacting against meritocracy it entrenches mediocracy. Regardless of nepotism it is sublimely self-perpetuating. Autocrats
relied on hand-picked cabinets and personal assistants. If they
were badly chosen, folly, incompetence and injustice could
flourish more luxuriantly than today. If they were well chosen,
efficiency triumphed. Though the system might not see itself as a
benevolent despotism, efficiency often brought general prosperity. Its rulers did not need to be loved for their little human
foibles but sought to be respected for their great human achievements. When government is by councils, committees and clusters
of bureaucrats all jealously watching one another for tinges of
individuality, there may be little malversation. There is also
likely to be little inspiration. The final result is not necessarily
an overall deterioration, but the disappearance of both the worst
and the best, that is, mediocracy in its literal sense.

In other fields mediocracy emerges in every sense, like anthills
on a barren plain. For while politics is the art of the possible,
other activities are the arts of the impossible. While politics is the
universal science, required to give something to everyone, other
pursuits are specialist sciences followed, in the first instance, for
their own sake and by their own devotees. A committee may
make a good administrative decision; it is unlikely to make a
good architectural or literary or musical decision. Yet in our
modern mediocracies, liberated from systematic analysis of conceptual principles, from private patrons or masterful maestros,
committee decisions are everywhere triumphant. One must not
seek a vision but a committee compromise. A sense of achievement is replaced by the sense of the meeting.

The feudal system is not the only system to collapse in our
pursuit of social justice. What feudalism was on a national scale
imperialism was on an international scale. The colonial power
regulated trade, investment, defence and government in an orderly
system, chiefly for its own convenience and its own profit. In
return it offered guaranteed markets, development of resources,
protection and civil order. Under this umbrella the colonies could
use opposition to foreign exploitation as a rallying-point in
coalescing their own factions prior to gaining emancipation and
possible expropriation of alien assets.

However long they flourished or monolithic they once seemed,
empires can be seen in retrospect as essentially unstable, tran-
sitional. As in a nuclear family the children eventually grow up,
rebel, leave home. They may not be happy; their parents may

fret. At least in the short term the fluttering brood will tear their wings while their parents flap behind in the nest, impotent, status-less, alone. It is an inevitable process bringing inevitable pain. But properly structured and timetabled its pain can be minimised and its inevitability acknowledged. New relationships can evolve into a new and less lopsided harmony, but only if there is time and patience and goodwill. In an atmosphere of 'liberty, equality, fraternity' – however understandable and just the cry may be – translated into popular consciousness, there is seldom time or patience or goodwill. In many countries the feudal system decayed bloodlessly without that cry, though religious wars often hastened the decay. Every modern empire has, however, collapsed in a bedlam of sound and a shower of blood, as imperial mediocrities who consistently failed to read danger signals were overthrown by colonial mediocrities who could read nothing else. In all too many cases a *pax Britannica* has been followed by a *bellum barbarum*.

Outside issues of local or global politics, there has been a more general, though less documented, collapse of systems. For centuries there flourished in theology, philosophy, ethics, natural science, law and other basic disciplines a belief in a systematic moral order in the universe. There might be controversy over how it was sustained and how it applied to the complex business of life, but theists and deists, atheists and agnostics, scientists and non-scientists, lawyers and laymen all persisted in a conviction that the universe was explicable in formal terms. The basic principle might be theistic teleology, or deistic entelechy, or scientific evolution – each with a clear (if, to mortal men, unclear) purpose in achieving an inbuilt potential. While each generation looked through a glass darkly at the infinite wonders of creation, it had satisfaction in knowing that it had cleared a little more of the glass and bequeathed to its successors a slowly expanding view.

Today this view is wider than ever before, clearer than ever before. Yet it is not the view anyone wants to look at. The principle of determinacy has been replaced by the principle of indeterminacy, the certainty principle by the uncertainty principle. There does not appear to be any cosmic purpose, divine or mundane. Moral law looks as fictional as natural law and the Decalogue less substantial than ten-pin bowling.

To those with imagination and insight, these discoveries have been liberating experiences. Rationalists have been right to shout them from the rooftops, even if they have failed to notice that rationalism itself is an intellectual system which has collapsed with all the others. At first sight the new learning might seem a breakthrough for meritocrats. No more can medieval mediocrats dilate to rapt audiences upon how many angels can perch on the head of a pin. No more can a Ptolemy or an Aristotle unleash formulae that strangle scientific observation for two millennia. The stagnant tyranny of systems is finished.

Unfortunately, the outcome has been a triumph for mediocracy rather than meritocracy. If intellectualism and rationalism may lead to tyranny, so too may empiricism and instrumentalism. If absurd conclusions can be drawn from systems, more absurd conclusions can be drawn from a systemless anarchy. No modern theologian has made anything like the contribution to his subject – mythical as it may be – of his medieval counterparts, and solid references to their preoccupation with angelic acrobats are hard to come by. Optical systems (replacing intellectual systems in astronomy) may produce optical illusions, and electron microscopes, cloud chambers, mass spectrometers and other aids to modern scientific research offer rich material for 'observations' that accord with religious beliefs, pet theories, published papers, research projects, faculty fetishes or strained eyes. Now that the universe as a whole does not 'make sense', trendy experimenters are under no obligation to 'make sense' of any of their 'findings' in terms of accepted knowledge in other fields, reason, commonsense, logic, biological purpose or any other yardstick that might once have cut the incredible down to size. So now we have, on the basis of some rarefied experiment, respectable claims for particulate freewill, anti-matter, negative time, infinite dimensions and inverted space. It is hardly surprising that scientists of lesser orthodoxy are moving in on witches, poltergeists, Martians, demons and clairvoyants.

The fact is that people are not accepting a systemless universe. Some are clinging obstinately, and in spite of all the evidence, to the old systems. What they cannot accept by reason they will accept by faith. If there is no new evidence to adduce they will accept the old evidence, dragged out and dressed up in modern language by the mediocrats who serve this sagging market. Other people, believing themselves liberated, are accepting new systems and greater tyrannies based on personal whim, successful charlatanry, idle speculation or downright fraud. If they cannot gain certainty from theologians they will gain it from *gurus*. They rise from psychiatrists' couches to sink on the couches of scientologists. They abandon doctors' surgeries for faith-healers' parlours. If they cannot find prophecies in the Bible they will find them in the stars.

As 'expediency', 'experimentation' and 'innovation' take the place of systems in politics, science and the arts, no mediocrat need fear unemployment. For, even if the public demanded meritocrats, where there is no acknowledged standard there can be no acknowledged merit. And where there is no acknowledged merit there is little incentive to strive, to create, to perfect. This is also a consequence of the collapse of another system, which began in the 1920s and is all but universal today. This is the monetary system. Now, it is rightly said that systems should be made for man and not man for systems; it is pointed out that attempts to return to a pre-war 'gold standard' after the Napoleonic Wars and the First World War led to disastrous consequences for workers and consternation among farmers; statistics show that from the rise of capitalism in the sixteenth century there have been cycles of boom and recession super-imposed on an overall inflationary trend; and debasement of coinage, by reducing the amount of precious metal in it, is as old as the Roman Empire. Nevertheless, until the twentieth century a belief persisted that, save for the upheavals of war throughout history and a bursting of speculative bubbles in the eighteenth century, national and international finance should operate on a fiduciary basis. If it were necessary to replace barter or cash payment with credit, its terms should be precise and constant. Currency should normally have a steady convertibility to other currencies and a stable purchasing power within its sphere of negotiability. Whatever views the Vatican might hold – till the sixteenth century – on usury, thrift was to be regarded as a virtue meriting reward. To compensate a lender for forgoing the pleasure of spending his savings, interest should be paid. The longer money was borrowed the higher the interest it should attract; and when the debt was finally liquidated, principal and interest should together be worth more than the original borrow-ing in real terms. Now all this has changed.

Treasurers no longer deem it necessary to balance their budgets or nations to live within their means. Deficit financing and currency devaluations are so common and so supported by academic economists, businessmen and trades unionists alike, that they have taken on the guise of a 'new morality'. No idle employer should not make a profit; no idle employee should be unemployed. Lenders should be content with interest less than the inflation rate, and the longer they are willing to lend, the less interest they should get. Overseas holders of currency should cheerfully see its value change overnight (when the money markets are closed) and small savers should not complain if their hard-won capital shrinks before their eyes. Big savers are less unfortunate as they have access to the high interest rates of the short-term money market, to downtown real estate speculation, to hoarding of gold, legally or illegally, to accumulation of diamonds, antiques, old masters or old port, to currency or commodity speculation and any other fashionable wrinkle that further debauches currency and undermines credit. Specific effects of this junketing, like housing crises and lost elections, cause momentary comment, but few commentators give a passing thought to the total undermining of confidence in political and economic systems that has resulted round the world. Particular victims are the lower middle classes, traditional upholders of stability, thrift, commitment to the future, people who normally fear to speculate and now fear even more to save. While media mediocrats continue to write of the Bomb, or 'alienation' in an industrial society, or disillusion with the nuclear family, or contempt for admass, as the chief provoker of *Weltschmerz*, economic insecurity is the real preoccupation of most people.

This economic insecurity may be more enervating than actual economic hardship, though on a world scale international organisations, aid and trade have done little for the masses in the Third World, where insecurity all too often lives side by side with hardship. Blame has been laid on multinational corporations, international speculators and corrupt politicians – and there is no dearth of guilty shoulders. Yet in many cases they seem to be reacting rather than acting, to be swept along in an irresistible tide with everyone else, and simply to be more successful at keeping their heads above water. Whatever moral judgement should be passed upon them, it is clear that they are people who are buoyant rather than brilliant, who are happy to devote their lives to money instead of the opportunities for improvement and self-improvement it can bring, who thrive on the brink of anarchy. For 'the disintegration of a system of rule is historically

reflected in the debasement and disappearance of its money'.[1]
And whoever would debauch a nation – or the world – need only
debauch its currency.

Whether runaway inflation is caused chiefly by demand-pull or
cost-push pressures is an academic question which the
mediocrats of economics seem unable to resolve when they are
willing even to consider it; for it presupposes importance in the
human factor, and many economists, Marxist and non-Marxist,
are happy to talk of their subject as if it consisted entirely of
impersonal forces. Both demand-pull and cost-push pressures
are, however, by-products of expectations: expectations of
improved living standards or expectations of further inflation.
'Liberty, equality, fraternity' has not thrown up liberty or
equality or fraternity but a medley of contending pressure groups
appealed to by mediocratic demagogues who pretend that living
standards can rise without rising gross national product, production can rise without increased productivity, incomes can rise
without effort or inflation. The result is that politicians have
become the worst sorts of pragmatists and electors the worst
sorts of floating voters. One principle survives: the principle of
mediocracy.

[1] G. K. Young, 'The Evolution of Change and Credit', in *New Humanist*,
London, February 1974.

CHAPTER FIVE

Decline and Fall of the Intellectual

'In his decline and fall the intellectual was probably pushed, but he chose to turn his descent into a dive.... Economic worries and the growing distractions and complexities of life subvert the position of an intellectual whatever his background or occupation.'

In 1959 one of the eight groups identified in British society was the intellectuals.

They are to be found in the teaching professions, both at schools and universities, in the Civil Service, in journalism, the liberal professions, and the arts. They are rational in their outlook and are generally still hopeful that they can participate in the development of a better world.... The phenomenon of their existence as a group at all is comparatively recent; for, for a long time, the idea of an English intelligentsia, with standards and habits of their own, was considered impossible, suspect and continental; at present, however, their position, derived from an increasing flow of graduates from the universities who are not, as in the past, inevitably absorbed by one of the other sections of the community, is likely to become more and more prominent.[1]

By 1968 an English-educated Indian *guru* told a group of Indian intellectuals:

Most of us are becoming, I am afraid, more and more

[1] Hugh Thomas's introductory essay, 'The Establishment and Society', in *The Establishment*, p. 12.

mediocre. We are not using that word in any derogative sense at all, but merely observing the fact of mediocrity in the sense of being average, fairly well educated, earning a livelihood and perhaps capable of clever discussion; but this leaves us still bourgeois, mediocre, not only in our attitudes but in our activities.[1]

Now, it might be thought that the differences between Madras and London, Hindu and Christian origins, individual temperaments and personalities, are more significant than the passage of nine years. On closer examination, however, the time gulf may seem all-important. Not that intellectualism was surging ahead in 1959 and careering backwards in 1968. No historical events could explain so dramatic a reversal. The difference is largely one of interpretation; the reversal, a psychological change from a position of basic optimism to one of basic pessimism. Adverse external events have supervened, but their impact is marginal. The crisis of confidence is largely internal.

While such crises are always subjective, at some stage there is a link with objective reality. If a former optimism and a later pessimism do not accurately reflect external changes, the explanation lies in changing physiology or interpretations. Where modified attitudes involve groups rather than individuals, the variant is interpretations, not physiology. These interpretations touch on reality. If it has undergone little change, either the original optimism or the later pessimism is unfounded.

This labouring of the obvious has been rendered necessary by the rise of the mediocracy, which induces two broad psychological reactions of its own. In undermining balanced judgement it magnifies moods, inducing ever wilder reactions and counter-reactions. Then, dimly aware of its pendulum effect, it invokes the theory of relativity to discount this effect. Interpretations vary, it claims, because no two individuals are ever the same and no single individual is the same from moment to moment, or because different people use language in a different way to make a gulf of meaning, not of viewpoint. Either there has been no external change or we have no way of knowing whether there has been. One interpretation is as good as any other, and if it chances to be pessimistic today it may be optimistic tomorrow. By this *reductio ad absurdum* any analysis of trends is undercut.

[1] J. Krishnamurti, *The Awakening of Intelligence*, London, 197 3, p. 2

This attitude may alone be ample demonstration of the decline and fall of the intellectual, but further evidence can be adduced. Like other measures of the modern world, his fall may be traced from the eighteenth century; but unlike some of them, it is part of a cyclical pattern with many earlier peaks and troughs. While there never seems to have been a cult of the 'common man' before our own, intellectuals have risen, declined and fallen before. Comparison of the mental climates of the Dark Ages and the Renaissance must discourage any historicist desire to predict permanent eclipse for the intellectual from now on, though his prognosis is hardly promising.

By 1958–9 all the signs of his latest decline and fall were glaringly obvious to the careful observer, almost as obvious as today. But superficial factors and misleading statistics obscured the casual view. These statistics were largely educational. As students and teachers were equated with 'intellectuals' and there was clearly a school and university explosion round the world, the number and influence of intellectuals were glibly assumed to be growing, indeed exploding. Moreover, in the highest echelons of learning there was the emergence of florid 'phudding' – the growth of PhD theses – without reference to whether this industry was either worthy or wanted. At the same time, in almost every field where talent or instinct or experience had hitherto flourished there appeared a mushroom growth of 'experts' nurtured beyond the confines of the classical university, yet equally beyond the university of hard knocks. Computer technology was making one of its many comebacks since the days of Leibniz, and the media mediocrats were apportioning the world among the intellectual titans who could talk to computers. Above all, in an age which judged everything by money, the rising cost of education was adduced as evidence of educational, hence intellectual, advance. 'Educational expenditure rose from 3.2 per cent of the Gross National Product in 1954 to 6.5 per cent in 1970. For the first time the nation was spending more on education than on defence.'[1] Need anything more be said? Few asked two further questions. Is more education the same as better education? Is education an extension of intellectualism or an extension of employment?

If there has in fact been a decline and fall of the intellectual since the eighteenth century, the reasons are divers and diverse.

---

[1] Anthony Sampson, *The New Anatomy of Britain*, London, 1971, p. 125.

The rise of democracy and the collapse of systems have contributed. For an intellectual deals in values which have never been popular and are increasingly vulnerable. The eighteenth century was an 'Age of Reason' because those who valued reason were socially, if not politically, influential and because reason held impeccable academic credentials. So greatly have these factors declined that the twentieth century might well be called an 'Age of Unreason'. In recent years deflation of reason appears to have gained momentum, but largely because the balloon has been almost airless since the First World War.

Origins of this deflation lie firmly in the eighteenth century itself, with the cult of Rousseau and the revolutionary cry of 'liberty, equality, fraternity'. Through Rousseau's discovery – or invention – of the 'noble savage' in a state of 'nature' many liberal intellectuals believed, and continue to believe, that they had rehabilitated pre-Christian 'fallen man' from the ruin of 'original sin' into which the clergy had cast him. In the event, Christians were not convinced while non-Christians went on to far more radical challenge of the Christian thesis. But Rousseau survived in another guise: in a populist suspicion of education and reason. 'Spontaneity' and 'emotion' and 'romanticism', which had been crowded out of the rationalist calendar by calculation, ratiocination and classicism, came in as feast days and soon became perennial. 'Liberty, equality, fraternity' was believed by the same liberal intellectuals to have libertarian implications alone. Only slowly has its anti-intellectualism evolved, stimulated by other forces and personalities. Søren Kierkegaard replaced futile theological debate on man's 'essence' with futile existentialist debate on his 'existence', and in the process bypassed steps of reason by a 'leap' of faith. This was on ground already softened by Immanuel Kant's unstable rationalist position that theism could not be proved by 'pure' reason though it could appeal to 'practical' reason. Like Kierkegaard, Thomas Huxley was a nineteenth-century figure who built on the eighteenth. His 'agnosticism' flowered where David Hume had watered. Though it was intended to discount esoteric claims to knowledge – gnosticism – of ultimate reality, it was soon transmuted to a popular view that nothing of any importance could be known at all and one man's 'opinion' was as good as any other's. This was endorsed in the nineteenth and twentieth centuries by the philosophy of pragmatism ('truth is what works') and the extension of the theories of evolution and relativity to social and philosophical subjects. At the same time psychology fragmented into the cults of the conditioned reflex, behaviourism and psychoanalysis: warring factions that united only to challenge the view of man as a rational being with an intellectual identity.

Today the delta of these streams of thought is clearly taking shape. In the words of one modern poet:

> I have been observing the world for about half a century and during that time it seems to me that something rather alarming has been happening: a progressive and, I fear, an accelerating loss of faith in reason which leads in turn to active contempt for rational thought and reasonable behaviour and a cultivation of the irrational and the perverse in its place.... I know I am hearing the voice of a generation which has lost its faith that there is a rational order in the world and that mankind, by courage and persistence, is itself rational enough to deal with it. I am talking about ... the failure of nerve: a tendency to run away from problems, I imagine, because one is afraid that they cannot be solved. There are plenty of young people today in the world as there were when I was young actively trying to set the world to rights. There always has been in the past. But something quite new is the even larger number of young people who want to 'drop out'.... Now this is only one aspect of a growing anti-intellectual movement in our time which manifests itself in many ways but particularly in a contempt for the past in history, in art, in society and even in science.... The other side of this failure of nerve is the increase of superstitions and superstitious practices masquerading as sciences. Dying pieces of nonsense like astrology, numerology, black magic and witchcraft, which one would have expected to wither away with the increase of knowledge and the spread of education, have gained a new lease of life and new sorts of nonsense like scientology have been springing up. It is as though many people were no longer able to tell the rational from the absurd because they don't want to. They prefer nonsense to sense.... The real crisis of this age, I believe, lies not in any specific problems such as the atom bomb or overpopulation or the destruction of the environment but in the fact that the greatest adventure of all time, the adventure of reason, is now threatened by its own

partial success – by a growing tendency to retreat now into barbarism.[1]

In other words, the decline and fall of the intellectual has accompanied the decline and fall of intellectualism.

Despite the collapse of the intellectual interpretation of history, intellectuals might have persisted as an hereditary privilegentsia adorning rather than informing society, like some ceremonial brigade of guards. Indeed, in the socialist countries this has become the role of compliant members of the intelligentsia. More active spirits rebel to smuggle out their self-pity or escape into the ocean of Western irrelevance, where they splash about for a while in a froth of political and religious commercialism before sinking into the great depths of public apathy. Oblivious of worldwide trends, one Soviet dissident has asked:

> Can a nation ever recover after it has ground into dust and destroyed whole generations, thereby stifling the intellect and condemning itself to collective loss of memory for further generations? ... No one should lightly dismiss our experience, as complacent foreigners do, cherishing the hope that with them – who are so clever and cultured – things will be different.... The experience we have had is the only thing that can give immunity – like a vaccine or inoculation.[2]

Trahison des clercs, the author implies, can anywhere lead to Stalinism – or to Nazism. It is, however, much to be doubted whether scholars were ever so important, and they have certainly not been so in the twentieth century, where they serve rather than cause tyranny. Yet there is truth in the claim that, in a broader context, 'destruction and self-destruction are the inevitable consequences of licence', that intellectuals have contributed to their own decline by a nihilistic debunking of all traditional standards and values. Could modern art and music have sunk so low if they had not been weighted down by the meaningless purple passages of mediocratic critics? Psychologists have been most expert at discrediting psychology; philosophers, philosophy; poets, poetry. In his decline and fall the intellectual was probably pushed, but he chose to turn his descent into a dive. If

[1] A. D. Hope, 'Guest of Honour', Radio 2FC (Australian Broadcasting Commission), Sydney, 24 December 1972.
[2] Nadezhda Mandelstam, *Hope Abandoned; A Memoir,* London, 1974, pp. 163, 617.

he looked up at the clifftop he would see his pushers. They are mediocrats rather than tyrants.

In the so-called liberal democracies the intellectual is caught up in another cyclical process. As he loses social and political power he loses income and status; and as he loses income and status he loses social and political power. Without asking what claim to intellectuality may fairly be laid by those groups called 'intellectuals' in *The Establishment* – teachers, civil servants, journalists, members of the liberal professions and the arts – one can see that in an inflationary age they are losing out as income-earners relative to other social groups and sometimes in absolute terms. If one sees an intellectual not as an 'expert' or 'specialist', administrator or educator, but as a source of creative ideas, it is clear that he is suffering even more. Survival as a freelance without private means is all but impossible and prospects for remunerative employment, or advancement within such employment, extremely limited. In education, government, journalism, 'liberal professions' (increasingly difficult to define) and the arts, a great deal of effort is devoted to projects that a little thought might have shown to be not worth pursuing, but no intellectual is thanked for pointing this out. Even in conservative countries intellectuals may now, in theory, emerge from all classes and castes and find their way into all power structures and professions. In practice, economic worries and the growing distractions and complexities of life subvert the position of an intellectual whatever his background or occupation.

The middle-class revolution of the nineteenth century threw up for a time an influential *nouveau-riche* contingent of *rentiers* who lived comfortably off their investments in stocks, bonds and property. Yields were steady, taxation minimal and inflation negligible. The 'year of revolutions', 1848, left most of them unscathed and thereafter, despite periodic demonstrations in the hearts of great cities, political stability shone on them for the rest of the century. In radical literature of their own and subsequent generations they have not cut too pretty a figure: smug, prim, parasitic, nepotistic. The hereditary privilegentsia they have spawned off would increasingly have attracted adverse comment on its genetic regression had not the class itself shrunk to insignificance outside the literary gossip columns. But what is often overlooked is that in its heyday it abounded in scholars and artists, philosophers and philanthropists. Relieved of domestic duties, regular commuting and economic insecurity, they were able to devote their lives to literary output, self-programmed and self-financed scientific research, scholarly contemplation and unpaid public service. The '400 families' left an intellectual legacy of which they are justly proud.

Changing economic factors have made a different climate today. If intellectuals were in high fashion, intellectualism would be difficult. While there is no dearth of very rich people who are richer today than ever before, their disposable income is a fraction of their nominal assets. Moreover, they are, on the whole, a very different set from the nineteenth-century *rentiers*. With graduated taxation and levies on capital gains, and with floods of Eurodollars and petrodollars washing round the world in and out of various currencies, commodities, speculative real estate, antiques, art, jewellery, equities and *vertu* (most of which are without either equity or virtue save the cash you can get for them from day to day), making and keeping money has become a fulltime job. However many people may be employed in preserving private fortunes, understandable resentment at vast economic inequalities in a supposedly egalitarian society and a steady erosion of fiduciary relationships at all levels of society are such that the affluent spend most of their time keeping an eye on their lawyers, accountants, butlers, valets and anyone else whose hand might be within reach of their diversified tills. Such a plutocrat is unlikely to have taste, and will certainly lack leisure, for creative activities of his own. Unlike the pre-*rentier* generation of aristocrats, who might themselves have been illiterate, he is unlikely to be a patron of the arts. Certainly he will buy manuscripts and paintings but only on the advice of his investment consultants and usually from artists who are dead. If job vacancies for contemporary plutocrats were advertised the successful candidate might well be described as suspicious, grasping, tasteless, fly, amoral and monomaniac ('sincerely wanting to be rich'[1]). However brilliant he may be at high finance and tax evasion, in all intellectual and cultural matters he is likely to be both a mediocrity and a mediocrat, merely enriching other mediocrities. Perhaps he is best described as mediogenic.

For people without these talents but with some capacity, sustained or sporadic, for intellectuality, the present and the future look very different. If their creation is unsuccessful they go unpaid; if successful, they are taxed with scant regard for years of

[1] Charles Raw *et al.*, *Do you sincerely want to be rich? Bernard Cornfeld and IOS: an international swindle*, London, 1971.

preparation and failure. If they can manage to save, they dare not put their savings into a bank or Government bonds or any other fixed-interest security for fear of massive depreciation from inflation. If they try property, vintage wines, mining shares, off-shore funds, antique silver or anything else whose sudden boom offers a 'hedge against inflation', they are likely to get in on the wrong side of the peak or fall victim to the many reefs and sharks that infest these troubled waters. If they should make a capital gain they are rightly taxed on it; but if they make a capital loss – as is usually the case with small investors and smalltime speculators – they do not get a rebate. If they are forced into a regular job (and most intellectuals are, even if well-known), though their working hours may be shorter than in the past, their leisure time is increasingly eroded by commuting, shopping, form-filling, domestic chores and 'do-it-yourself' in essentially alien fields, repairing 'labour-saving' devices that are perpetually going wrong, car maintenance, gardening. There is no end to the distractions that beset 'middle-class intellectuals' today. Non-intellectual work can be computerised or system-atised in other ways and the workers benefit from the increased productivity. It is the very nature of intellectual work to be non-repetitive and beyond the genius of systems analysts. It is just as well that there is now little demand for intellectual effort, since a multitude of adverse factors have ensured that there is little of it forthcoming.

The intellectual might still flutter, chirruping to himself, in some ecological corner unknown to all but the most intrepid bird-watchers and pronounced extinct by scientific opinion. Alas, his ultimate eclipse is worse than this. Science has pronounced him non-existent. Distinguished pollsters and psephologists, sociologists and media researchers, who would never dream of conducting a mass survey on the best way of drilling a tooth or disposing of garbage – rightly believing that these are specialist matters where one man's opinion is not as good as another's – cheerfully resolve intellectual questions on impeccable egalitarian principles. Does God exist? Is Shakespeare relevant? Is the world drifting towards socialism? Is abortion socially desirable? Is the world overpopulated? – these and a thousand other complex subjects appear to need no other investigation than accosting in the street people whose minds are on shopwindows and traffic lights, who have seldom turned their attention to the issue put to them and who rarely have adequate background knowledge to make an informed judgement, jotting down their unpremeditated replies and totting up the totals. God in his heaven, Shakespeare and Marx in their graves and foetuses in their wombs tremble on the outcome. Full of some strange death-wish, liberal intellectuals have discovered not only that intellectual questions need neither knowledge nor experience in their assessment, but that no assessor has special talent for the task.

Underlying this issue is the assessment of intellect, which may best be defined as an interest and facility in the solution of abstract or philosophical problems. With the decline and fall of the intellectual, however, such problems are deemed to be either incapable of solution or not worth solving. So the 'mental' phenomenon that has superseded intellect is 'intelligence'. Were education not big business desperate, with the decline of formal examinations, for some assessment of profitability, one would not have heard too much about intelligence. But it is here and trendily controversial. Now, it is true that many intelligence tests are devised by mediocrats who would themselves starve on a desert island where the dunce of the school would thrive; that is, they are assessing ability in problem-solving which seems to be related more closely to the cultural background of the tester than to the needs of the real world. That said, intelligence tests are being increasingly refined and are clearly measuring something independent of cultural background, for siblings – save identical twins – in the same family record different scores. They also have different heights, weights, colouring and other physical characteristics, and these are on all sides acknowledged to be genetically determined. And just as individuals vary in their bodily characteristics, so too do average specimens of different races, again on genetic grounds. Physically, there is less evidence for the equality of man than of any other species, and liberal intellectuals never cease to glory in the size, strength and agility of the negroid races. Yet professors can get assaulted by university students for asserting 'the inequality of man'[1] in a mental sense, overwhelmingly confirmed by testing of individuals and ethnic groups, analysis of intellectual output throughout history and simple observation of one's contemporaries.

It is easy to see that such observations are politically sensitive and educationally embarrassing, and it should be constantly

[1] H. J. Eysenck, *The Inequality of Man*, London, 1973.

pointed out that within each group there is a broader spread of differences of measured intelligence than among the norms for all the groups. Nevertheless, denial of obvious intellectual inequality cannot benefit either politics or education. It can benefit only the mediocracy.

CHAPTER SIX

Collapse of Authority

'While people can stagnate within an ordered society, such a state has always been a precondition of all that makes civilisation: harmony, predictability, assurance, creativity. . . . Upheavals make rich soil for demagogues; chaos fertilises mediocre demagogues.'

It may at first sight seem surprising to relate the rise of the mediocracy to a postulated collapse of authority and date the origins of both to the eighteenth century. For that was a time when, by contrast with our own, to travel the highways by day or night, singly or in company, armed or unarmed, was to invite the attention of brigands; and this was as true of the 'civilised' countries as of the most primitive parts of the globe. Going to earlier centuries one discovers continents torn apart by contests between monarchs and pretenders, popes and anti-popes. If the highest offices in state and church were gained, held or lost by ephemeral advantage in a perpetual power struggle before the eighteenth century, how can a collapse of authority be dated to subsequent times?

The truth is that, if the concept of authority is firmly entrenched, a stable total situation can embrace a succession of apparently unstable regimes. Cracks in the body politic are hastily plastered over by new consecrations, anointings and oaths of allegiance which create a pleasing façade till the next explosion, so that while authorities are continually challenged, authority reigns supreme. This is the position that flourished till the eighteenth century, caught cold in the nineteenth and died in the twentieth.

Causes of the malady – if it is that and not a liberating experience – are similar to those precipitating the rise of democracy, collapse of systems and decline and fall of the intellectual. Diagnosis should not rest on the number of wars and civil wars, of uncrowned kings and incarcerated bishops (though they make an impressive list which is constantly renewed), but on philosophical and social attitudes of a more fundamental kind. Nor, despite the moralistic overtones of 'collapse of authority', should its symptomatology necessarily include the collapse of morality, which is 'a function of environmental influences and individual potentialities, multicentric in its points of growth'[1], and largely independent of political or religious authority.

Despite utopian socialist attempts of the early nineteenth century to equate the 'voice of God' and the 'voice of the people', with the disappearance of the divine right of kings there remained little evidence for the divine right of any other system of government. For a time the 'social contract' or 'natural law' or 'moral law' was elevated in its place, but while these are still sometimes invoked they are generally recognised as political fictions. In the eighteenth century there was an anxious effort to avert atheism by enthroning the god of deism on the seat vacated by the discredited god of theism, coupled with aristocratic determination not to discuss religion critically in front of the servants. But the god of deism did not rule long into the nineteenth century, while those lucky enough to have servants today do not discuss religion in front of them so as not to bore them. Long after genuine belief in established institutions of state and church had evaporated, an inflow of tradition filled the vacuum. But tradition depends on the authority of custom, and that too collapsed when the theories of evolution and relativity became multi-disciplinary. Though elusive in the concrete, the beautiful, the good and the true had for centuries been thought absolute in the abstract; but now they too became relative. At the same time, moral philosophers rediscovered Hume's anxiety over how to pass from 'is' statements to 'ought' statements and declared the attempt to be a 'naturalistic fallacy'. The authority of ethics as a normative discipline collapsed and, in the hands of men who were neither linguists nor littérateurs, it graduated from being a study of morality to becoming a study of the language of morality. In the absence of intellectual authority, the authority of

1 David Tribe, *Nucleoethics: Ethics in Modern Society*, London, 1972, p. 206.

teachers and of the whole educational system found itself base-
less and toppled into the abyss. If prelates, princes, priests and
pedagogues lacked natural credentials, who could any longer give
credence to paterfamiliases? Not that it mattered, for the family
itself was declared a monstrous anachronism. Since all behaviour
was relative, psychiatry and penology were comparable tyrannies, whose power of the keys was as bogus as St Peter's. Indeed,
so suspect has their authority become that it is solemnly pro-
claimed that the only sane people are inside mental hospitals and
the only virtuous ones inside prison cells. No one should be
arrested save policemen and no one imprisoned save prison
officers.

How then should life be lived in a world where authority is
dead? Will forced obedience to a stratified society yield to glad
participation in an egalitarian society? Will the tyranny of
tradition sink beneath the cradle of creativity? Is 'freedom now'
the recipe for a gentle loving anarchy? It does not appear to be
so. The suzerainty of the bourgeoisie must succumb to the
dictatorship of the proletariat; today's power structure to Black
Power, Student Power, Pupil Power, Gay Power, Cunt Power.
Revolution must overthrow the 'system' and perpetual revolution renew the revolution. 'Politics comes out of the barrel of a
gun' has become not just a counsel of expediency but a great
moral principle. The power of the press should collapse before the
power of the underground press; society before the alternative
society; culture before the counter-culture. In our concern for the
environment, the blackboard jungle should be protected like any
other jungle. All activity should be declared alienating save the
unspecified activity of 'activists'. Everything should attract
protest save the protest movement. Freedom fighters must cherish
every freedom save that of innocent bystanders to stay alive. In a
world of scepticism and gratuitous psychoanalysis, the only
people whose motives can be pronounced stainless are guerrillas
and urban guerrillas, hijackers and skyjackers. Where admass
promotes detergents it is evil; where it promotes the *gurus* and
arbiters of popular taste it is good. Fashion is to be decried only
if it is high fashion, demagogues only if they are right-wing,
revolutions only if they are counter-revolutions. Between revolutions one should work at one's play and play at one's work.

If this analysis is correct one might after all be inclined to
formulate a law of the conservation of authority: authority can
neither be created nor destroyed, it can only be changed. Glad-

stone had something like this in mind when he declared: 'Those who think lightly of the testimony of the ages, the tradition of their race, which at all events keeps them in communion with it, are often found the slaves of Mr A or Mr B, of their newspaper or of their club.'[1] A modern writer has set this theme in a context of mediocracy:

> When the rich and the powerful are falsely modest and afraid of colour and splendour, the whole style of life deteriorates – there being no example to follow save that of cultivated mediocrity. High style and pageantry are then confined to the theatre, and – being left out of all such serious domains as religion, government, and commerce – become signs of frivolity, with the disastrous result that seriousness (or, better, sincerity) must always be associated with a drab aspect.[2]

When mediocrity is cultivated it becomes a mediocracy, wielding its own kind of power and exercising what some might call a new authority. It is a matter of definition, but 'authority' is perhaps best reserved for an influence which has, as its derivation suggests, a precise originator and sustainer, power base and ideological superstructure, past, present and future. This does not mean that authority is necessarily benevolent and much of it is not. That the rule of imperious princes, prelates, priests and parsons has been diminished will be greeted on most sides with relief. That parents and teachers are no longer martinets, or children the passive potter's clay of their desires, will be welcomed by most societies. Yet, like other social forces, authority is subtly interrelated with the dynamics of living. Periodically it needs to be redirected; never should it be occluded.

Though traditional authorities were often both mystical and mythical, they flourished because they commanded belief or compelled allegiance. In their time-honoured trappings they gained a potency that was not intrinsic and could inspire even when they were not inspirational. Under this mantle the talented took on new dimensions and even the mediocre lost some of their flatness. They may have owed their position to suspension of disbelief, but suspension of disbelief can be as good as belief.

[1] W. E. Gladstone, 'On the Influence of Authority in Matters of Opinion', in *The Nineteenth Century*, London, March 1877.
[2] Alan Watts, *In My Own Way: An Autobiography 1915–1965*, London, 1973, p. 7.

When there is a concept of authority, diversified society takes on a semblance of order. Eventually a semblance of order becomes order. While people can stagnate within an ordered society, such a state has always been a precondition of all that makes civilisation: harmony, predictability, assurance, creativity. Revolutions which occur in corrupt communities may form the basis of a new and improved order. Until that order is established, nothing of substance emerges. Unless the leaders of revolution have internal order, within themselves and within the revolutionary brotherhood, nothing of substance will ever emerge. Revolution for the sake of revolution brings only chaos. Upheavals make rich soil for demagogues; chaos fertilises mediocre demagogues. As the human species gravitates to society, chaos is by definition unstable. Sooner or later the mediocrities who float on its surface coalesce as a mediocracy of a particularly nasty and vicious sort.

The collapse of authority we see around us is not to be gauged simply by the number of existentialist nonentities who become entities when they seize a petrol bomb. Nor is it measurable by statistics of crime and delinquency, vandalism and divorce, alcoholism and drugtaking. These things are important, but they happen in every war and civil war as part of its pattern of disintegration. (If they are directed against the enemy they are given more heroic labels.) Most commented on is the collapse of political authority, which is more significant than the collapse of political authorities. Yet in the last analysis there may be more significant tokens of collapse.

Rebellion against the 'old men' of the Cabinet or the boardroom may be justified; rebellion against old age is a rebellion against values of wisdom, experience, stability, continuity and balance which are abandoned with temerity. Collapse of systems does not stop at the collapse of the feudal system or the capitalist system or any other political structure of dubious value. Unchecked, this collapse soon overtakes the educational system and the legal system, and soon we find we have lost application, apprenticeship, craftsmanship, humility before facts, initiative, equity (not to say equities), objectivity. The decline and fall of the intellectual involves more than clusters of increasingly maudlin *manqués* in progressively seedier and remoter bars. It involves the disintegration of rationality and belief in reason, creation and belief in creativity, vision and belief in informed viewpoints. Collapse of industrial authority means more than longer tea breaks and shorter tempers. It implies erosion of contractual obligations, job satisfaction and reliable workmanship. As, in the demonology of radical chic, there is no creature more vicious than the WASP (White Anglo-Saxon Protestant), so the collapse of traditional religion has particularly overtaken Protestantism and the 'Puritan ethic'. Happily, this development has undercut prudery, biblical fundamentalism and sabbatarianism. Less happily, it has also undercut the virtues of thrift, conscientiousness and effort. Work has become a bore and a chore. Well-paid assembly-line jobs are said to be soul-destroying and their end is called for. It is not specified whether the desired alternative is automation with unemployment or cottage industries with pauperism. In a world where most people are poor the horrors of the affluent society are regularly denounced by affluent *literati*. For the very rich, life itself has become a bore, though it is rendered more tolerable by organisations that will, for a fee, provide the experiences of simulated gangsterdom (if the actuality is not found more appealing), slavery or childhood.

It is possible to exaggerate contemporary 'alienation'. 'The fact that young workers are more insistently demanding a middle-class life style will hardly suggest, to the disinterested observer, that they are an "alienated" class. To reach such a conclusion, you have to be an "alienated" sociologist. Of these, alas, we seem to have an abundant supply.'[1] There is, however, something disturbing about a mediocracy seeking a middle-class life-style after abandoning the only values which have proved themselves able to deliver the goods.

[1] Irving Kristol, 'Workers of the World', in *The Australian Financial Review*, 25 January 1973.

C

CHAPTER SEVEN

Philias

'The philias have unsettled more people than they have liberated, seducing the able from constructive work or stable relations and promoting neurosis, fickleness, fecklessness and insecurity in all sections of society. . . . They provide ample opportunity for neurotic mediocrities to gain both notoriety and a martyr's crown.'

Since the eighteenth century there has been a mushrooming of all the philias, with the possible exception of necrophilia. In an age of dictated 'professionalism' it is natural that there should be a reaction towards the amateur, or 'lover', and in an age of tension and sexual neurosis it is healthy to 'make love, not war'. Inside the churches the God of justice has largely been replaced by the God of love and accordingly the newest New Theologians optimistically proclaim the 'ground of our being', which is God, as pure love. In so far as marriage is regarded as more than legalised prostitution or an occasion for dressing up and revelry, it has become less a passport to contractual obligations than a funfare ticket to romantic love.

Like motherhood before Women's Lib, love has traditionally been regarded as a 'good thing' whatever one's personal experiences. Few have dared to challenge it, lest they be labelled apostles of hate. Undoubtedly it can lead to uncomplaining service, warm sympathy and creative enthusiasm. Yet it can also be a destructive passion, undermining reason, commonsense, judgement and justice and fostering jealousy, possessiveness, passion and hate. Whether advocated by Christian or humanist sentimentalism – both commencing their onslaught on logic in the eighteenth century and triumphing in the twentieth – 'universal love' is particularly suspect. Unrelated to actuality it is a mere expression of feeling that may suddenly change if its anonymous recipients do not respond to unreasonable expectations of reciprocity; though it is frequently indulged with no regard whatever for I-thou responses, I-you responses or any responses at all. Not unusually it is a handmaiden of insensitive paternalism and bombast. 'I do not know if you have observed the violence all over the world. The younger generation were at first giving flowers to everybody, living in a world of "beauty" and imagination; when that did not work, they took to drugs, they became violent, and we are now living in a world of complete violence.'[1] It is not, therefore, necessarily reassuring when a whole generation lays claim to a philia.

For most of its evolution the human species has been agrarian. Most of the world's population is still agrarian. Peasants tend to be conservative. For most of history tradition has been important to mankind. Perhaps it has been too important. With that reassessment in mind, the most vocal members of the most vocal societies have sought to unseat tradition. Their aims have been worthy: the liberation of creative energies, the emergence of suppressed groups, the achievement of law reform. And much has been done. Yet increasingly 'neophilia', or love of new things, has become not a means to an end but an end in itself. The whole world of experience has become a crucible, with philia its flux. In it, liberated creative energies have drowned, emergent suppressed groups have been resubmerged, law reform has masked the law. Neophilia has been related to the myth of the sacrificial god-king who dies that his people may live. 'Here we are obviously touching on a complex of the most profound myths of the human race – the myth of the King who must die in order that a new King may reign; the myth of the Golden Bough; that the old year must die in order to give way to the new; the basic rhythm of the eternal renewal, not just of life but also of order, the framework in which alone life can be maintained.'[2] This myth has, however, traditionally taken care to stress continuity in novelty and life in death. 'The King is dead; long live the King!' In losing this continuity and not resurrecting this life, modern mythology has largely contributed to 'future shock',[3] where to most people in

---

[1] Krishnamurti, *The Awakening of Intelligence*, p. 296.
[2] Christopher Booker, *The Neophiliacs: a study of the revolution in English life in the Fifties and Sixties*, London, 1969, p. 328.
[3] Alvin Toffler, *Future Shock*, London and New York, 1970.

the 'civilised' world the future has ceased to look challenging and has become frightening. In some countries certain adventitious once-for-all changes like conversion to the metric system have cut all but the young adrift from a world of familiar values and measurements and left them floundering in a sea of strange names and unimaginable size. But this is a temporary stage and will, in the final analysis, shrink before endemic variability in many aspects of modern life.

Whether we stay at home or travel abroad, inflation and con-vertibility of currencies undermine 'values' and expectations until all values and all expectations seem to be threatened. For political reasons, place names seem to be continually changing, while gentility is wonderfully productive of new and misleading euphemisms for mundane jobs and unpleasant social phenomena. 'The rodent operative is taking advantage of temporary cooling of an overheated economy to undergo job retraining' means 'Depression has put the ratcatcher out of work'. In supposedly serious disciplines the collapse of intellectual authority and artistic standards has not brought real freedom but reckless 'experimentation' or an unstable trendiness. Instead of doing their work or doing their duty or doing their best in areas where all may know the rules and judge the outcome, the neophiliacs begin by 'doing their own thing' in a deontological void until, daunted by their own daring, they take up the fashion of the moment. Not surprising, therefore, that in the narrow worlds of fashion-wear and life-style, trends have changed faster than cybernetics can cope with, so that the end result is a chaos of eclecticism and the new 'scruffy' look. Planned obsolescence has made consumer 'durables' less durable, while continual changing of models and components is less productive of improved effi-ciency than of inability to get spare parts. Unstable trivia become intrusive by their instability, distracting the able from more serious pursuits and providing golden opportunities for successions of mediocrities.

With the collapse of authority and tradition has come the collapse of what used to sustain them: the natural authority of age. This could, and often did, become a gerontocracy but it enshrined qualities which cannot lightly be desecrated: wisdom, experience, maturity, balanced judgement. At all events we must now live without them, for gerontocracy has been replaced by juvenilophilia. Naturally there are areas like pop culture and design where the young in heart are likely to be young and where innovation is more important than maturity, but these areas are neither the most numerous nor the most important in life's landscape. Juvenilophilia has other disadvantages. Like gerontocracy, or sexism, or racialism, or any other arbitrary division, it fails to account for the range of human potentiality. Some young people show mature judgement, some old ones innovating flair. There is never so much talent around that it can be idly squandered – save in a mediocracy which neither recognises nor wants it. Unlike gerontocracy, juvenilophilia is often treated indulgently even when not adulated. 'I don't know why one has made such an extraordinary thing out of young people, why it has become such an important thing. In a few years they will be the old people in their turn.'[1] This indeed is the crux. It means that juvenilophilia is ultimately more enervating to both the individual and society than gerontocracy. For the acquisition of status as a grandparent or tribal elder gives something to aim for and look forward to. The great bulk of people are not teeny-bops. With modern medicine the proportion of the aged is steadily growing. Yet we are in the depressing situation where pop singers can wail that life has finished now that they are twenty-five. And, professionally, so it has. For promoters know that the pop market is among 15–25-year-olds, who like to identify with a famous contemporary; and as each 'old man' bows out at twenty-five to a life of future frustration there is another 'discovery' ready to leap into his shoes. Juvenilophilia was a particular feature of youthful 'outsiders' and 'angry young men' in the mid-twentieth century. Though some of them use every device of the cosmetician, wigmaker and boutique designer to create an illusion of perpetual youth, some of them are dimly aware that they are young no longer. If they have managed to hang on to prematurely acquired power they are naturally reluctant to relinquish it. So perhaps juvenilophilia will be less trumpeted for a while. But it retains a powerful hold on western societies. Despite brave talk, by Ministers for Employment round the world, of job retraining throughout life, 'too old at forty' or 'too old at thirty' is the familiar barrier to 'elderly' job hunters. If people don't 'make it' when they are young they doubt if they ever will. Old age has become a time to dread, a time of increasing irrelevance and, on retirement – if the old presume to live so long – of grave financial anxiety as inflation erodes fixed or

[1] *The Awakening of Intelligence*, p. 21.

sluggishly rising incomes. 'Alienation' for most people is not caused by the assembly-lines of multinational corporations or the jingles of advertising agencies, but by social attitudes bequeathed by the radical chic.

Subculture power groups – Black Power, Student Power, Pupil Power, Gay Power, Cunt Power – have proliferated so luxuriantly in recent years from reform groups going back into the eighteenth or nineteenth centuries that they may be designated as philias. Student Power and Pupil Power are by-products of juvenilophilia. Though it may operate in the name of any non-white group, Black Power is quintessentially negrophilia. Gay Power may be called homophilia and Cunt Power, somewhat ambiguously, gynophilia. No one can doubt but that these causes arose from genuine grievances which have not entirely vanished. There are still people and groups of people who trade in easy labels when confronted with the rest of humanity. If accepted, these labels are more than picturesque descriptions but passports to designated positions in society, regardless of individual needs or abilities. If the people labelled are minorities or traditionally quiescent groups, their designated positions are likely to be subservient. But will 'liberation' come from a philiac attitude?

History shows that, whatever label a group may be given, outstanding individuals within it can rise to influential positions if they play their cards well. Using their own people as a power base and appealing to the fear or the pity of ruling classes, they capitalise on their position during the vital early stages of any power struggle. Even slaves have been able to use their proximity to the great to their own advantage. This was particularly true under the old oligarchs, who, when they looked beyond their own families for promotable material, were often more impressed by personal observation or sexual liaison over a period than by recommendations from somebody else. It is ironic that today these minority groups borrow freely from Marxist jargon and claim the 'people's' struggle as their own, since the greatest obstruction to their advancement comes from the 'people' – the working classes and blue-collar unions – motivated by both lack of imagination and sectional self-interest. For this reason rather than because of establishmentarian bias they have not, in conventional terms, made much political progress, that is, gained many seats in elected assemblies. Yet even in modern democracies there are enough sympathetic members of majorities to help above-average representatives of minorities with scholarships and housing finance, while below-average individuals usually have access to welfare benefits. Indeed, often they receive more than comparably situated 'poor whites', thus adding to the resentment of the majority community. And, characteristically of modern society, majority or minority, whatever they receive is received ungraciously.

A proper analysis of each of these pressure-group philias – and the corresponding phobias – would be a book in itself. It would show difficulties experienced by poor non-whites in gaining jobs in certain service industries or moving into white suburbs; by students and pupils in gaining representation on decision-making bodies at any level in education; by homosexuals in seeking as free expression of their love as heterosexuals; by women in gaining entry to certain manual or administrative occupations or obtaining mortgages if they are single. Many unacceptable features of discrimination have been recognised for some time and were being eroded by traditional methods of law reform: pamphleteering, petitioning, lecturing, lobbying; in other words, appealing to reason and enlightened self-interest as well as humanitarianism. For solid reformist movements do not need to rely on emotion, much less on hysteria. Though they may appeal to idealism, they have excellent practical credentials. The socio-economic cost of denying reform can be shown to be bigger than that of granting it.

Once there was an evolution of reformism. Now, under the reign of media mediocrats, this too has its fashions and its fads. The Bomb is 'in' one year and 'out' the next. Ex-colonial demagogues and other factitious martyrs of the protest movement plummet overnight from celebrity less because they are discredited than because they are forgotten. Neophilia is no respecter of persons. It is now *avant-garde* to thrust women into the sorts of jobs that nineteenth-century reformers struggled to get them out of.

Behind many of today's philias, giving them a cohesiveness and community of interest they may at first sight seem to lack, are some basic features: unscientific arrogance before the facts, ignorance of or contempt for history, bogus egalitarianism, anti-intellectualism, hysteria, belief in instant solutions of complex problems, unwarranted generalisation from the particular. Consequently, a number of propositions of conventional wisdom (some of which were admittedly more conventional than wise) have been turned entirely on their heads. These giddy new dogmata cannot be considered entirely satisfactory. What should be accepted in a minority need not be recommended to a majority. What may be a legitimate part of youthful experimentation need not offer a suitable model for older age groups. What may be adventurous in the childless may be disastrous in a family situation. The philias have unsettled more people than they have liberated, seducing the able from constructive work or stable relations and promoting neurosis, fickleness, fecklessness and insecurity in all sections of society. Negrophilia and gynophilia have particularly aided the decline and fall of the intellectual, for they have discounted those qualities that negroes and women as historical groups have conspicuously lacked: inventiveness, scholarship, scientific and philosophical creativity, mathematical flair and logical problem-solving. Apologists insist that members of these groups have been traditionally deprived and dispirited, denied opportunities and forced into apathy. Prevailing social attitudes have not, however, prevented Negroes from becoming successful athletes and jazz musicians and women from flourishing as domestic novelists and watercolourists – even at times when such activities were discouraged. The question should be asked whether, on average, these groups have any basic talent in the fields where they have not shone. Of course the question is not asked, as this would undermine trendy egalitarianism. Above all, it might lead to further questions which could threaten the rule of the mediocracy.

Some less-than-rabid supporters of the philias may concede that their colleagues have sometimes overstated their arguments but justify this ploy on the grounds that only shock tactics can rouse the general public from its usual torpor and that law reform has thereby been advanced. Like most other philiac claims, this is a highly dubious proposition. A more convincing case may be made out to suggest that the contrary is true. In early stages of reformist campaigns there is a case for literary shocks, like Dickensian novels or Galsworthian plays, to force the genteel to consider, in a fictional context, aspects of life to which they have hitherto given scant attention. Forced confrontation with reality, or grotesque caricatures of reality, may negate rather than reinforce pangs of conscience.

Power-hungry philias have succeeded in confirming in the popular imagination stereotypes of minority groups that a lifetime of enlightened education by 'old-fashioned' reformers was starting to break down. Black Power has revived the 'big buck nigger' of malignant potential. Student Power and Pupil Power have refurbished the image of the 'lazy, long-haired layabout' pursuing any activity other than the studies he receives grants for. Gay Power has rescued the 'screaming queen' of vaudeville from exile and enthroned her again. Cunt Power – or Women's Lib – has reduced the drama of mankind's eternal quest for dignity to a farce of bra-burning and has satisfied every male chauvinist pig that a 'liberated' woman is either an embittered divorcee or a butch lesbian. Not content with alienating public opinion by creating florid images, these power groupers hail resort to violence as a legitimate way to woo support. They hardly cause more damage or bloodshed than gangs of hooligans (aristocratic in the Middle Ages and proletarian in ours) but it is done in the name of tolerance and justice and with the benefit of free publicity from the radical chic. Within the ranks of these movements are people of great sensitivity and dedication, but they provide ample opportunity for neurotic mediocrities to gain both notoriety and a martyr's crown.

If they have no taste for 'law reform', neurotic mediocrities are increasingly gaining other outlets for notoriety. One is psychedelic drugs. Another is 'encounter' or 'awareness' or 'sensitivity' groups.

Now, the real 'drug problem' of modern life is the growing dependence of respectable society on cigarettes, alcohol, analgesics, tranquillisers, sedatives and stimulants. In the eyes of the mediocratic media, however, it is the drug subculture revolving round hallucinogenic drugs. Alternate glamorisation and denunciation of this subculture have reinforced its natural narcissism and paranoia and unleashed a great literature of self-justification. It is as though souls in torment not only insisted on their inalienable right to go to hell but bombarded the living with unstamped postcards: 'Having wonderful time; wish you were here.' Life is intolerable, they say; walk out, pass through 'the doors of perception' and enter 'inner space'. Throughout history, usually associated with religion and sometimes with the arts, rare souls and precious idlers have sought mystical experience by a variety of techniques. The simplest and potentially most harmful of these is drugtaking – pharmacophilia – which has therefore gained the ascendancy. Its simplicity appeals to the mediocracy, its potential danger to those in search of 'kicks'. If no one else is harmed the issue should not be regarded as a moral one. There do, however, seem to be ample opportunities for harming others, while intellectual and aesthetic consequences are often overlooked.

Under the influence of drugs people can be just as unreliable and irresponsible as under the influence of drink. Victims of heroin withdrawal are half-crazed candidates for any sort of crime. Marijuana may cause chromosomal breakdown and congenital addiction to sundry hard drugs can be bequeathed to offspring – unless the female drugtaker has learned from Women's Lib that childbearing is degrading to the natural masculinity of women. While the 'dropout' settles back comfortably to enjoy whatever benefits of a Welfare State may be available, someone else who might be equally capable of 'beautiful' thoughts has to work to maintain it. Fortunately for the worker, the mediocracy's tolerance of perversion saves him from persecution for his disgusting addiction to work. Fortunately, too, he can read the beautiful and expensive thoughts of those who are translated to a hippie's heaven. If their repetitive sludge is indeed more sparkling than the creations of normal perception, under the benign influence of the mediocracy normality must be richly polluted.

Those who lack imagination or nerve to become drug addicts can gain instant experience through encounter groups. These usually meet in the nude and the more wholesome of them are probably refined orgies. Perhaps some individuals do gain catharsis from sexual or non-sexual multiple contact, from criticising and being criticised, from dressing down in public and dressing up in private, from screaming and weeping and groaning. Perhaps some organisers of these sessions have special psychological qualifications or talents to re-dress the emotionally naked in clothes more suitable than they entered in. Perhaps. In some cases intellectual streakers are offering raiment to emotional nudes. Even if they do not cause lasting harm to the unbalanced, they are merely presenting, at enormous expense (to their patrons, not to themselves), a theatre where the audience provides its own entertainment or a brothel where the clients bring their own prostitutes. But encounter groups should not be knocked. They provide copy for glossy magazines, theses for aspiring PhDs, research projects for psychologists and occupation for the mediocracy. Looking across the street at the drug-fertilised 'flower children' – cohorts of untrained Flower Power –

blossoming in infection and squalor, pimping and poncing, dreaming of Himalayan valleys in some urban canyon, members of encounter groups may even feel secure within their instability.

CHAPTER EIGHT

Rise of Technology

'In replacing the lone wolf of science by the hunting pack of production engineering, technology has brought deflation to individualists and elation to mediocrats. While providing jobs for the mediocracy, which has a special flair for filling places where talent might once have been expected, technology has exercised debilitating influence over us all.'

During the Second World War E. M. Forster found time to complain of 'the implacable offensive of science'.[1]

This implacable offensive has not arisen from its environment in a simple unilinear fashion as that stern determinist, Karl Marx, himself acknowledged. Its momentum, though owing much to what Max Scheler called 'real factors' – race, geopolitics, political power structures or the production machine – has increased by accretion. The aggregation of those sustaining the momentum – demonstrators of truths based on observable facts, or exploiters of trustworthy methods for discovering 'new truths' – has taken place as the offensive intensifies.[2]

The language of science and technology has become as formidable and fearsome as science and technology themselves.

Ever since the palaeolithic age technology has been rising, but it is only in the last hundred years that its ascent can be called meteoric. A number of factors are responsible. In western intellectual circles empiricism gained grudging acceptance as recently

[1] 'The New Disorder', in *Horizon*, Vol. IV (1941), pp. 379–80.
[2] W. H. G. Armytage, *The Rise of the Technocrats: A Social History*, London, 1965, p. vii.

as the seventeenth century, and there was a natural lag between the triumphs of pure science and those of applied science. Even more than in most information explosions, applied science tended to erupt exponentially, each new discovery leading to two more. As discoveries and applications extended in the fields of navigation and armaments, the entire power balance of the world was altered. Countries where the scientific revolution originated (outside China, which had experienced it much earlier and in virtual isolation) were relatively poor in natural resources, but their new-found technology enabled them to colonise lands which had what they lacked. With the rise of democracy came rising material expectations among classes that had not hitherto been noted for conspicuous consumption. For a while, then, in the second half of the nineteenth century and the first half of the twentieth, economic growth, increased purchasing power, discoveries of raw materials and processes to exploit them advanced in overall balance. By the second half of the twentieth century it was obvious that the balance was toppling. (This is one disharmony which cannot be attributed to the decline and fall of the intellectual, since the previous harmony was largely fortuitous.) Medical technology was accelerating death control beyond birth control, while the phenomenon of rising expectations spread from the First to the Second and Third Worlds. At the same time, the earth's capacity to respond to growing demands was shown to be finite in practice as well as in theory. One had to be intrepid indeed to find unexplored lands or virginal continental shelves. Rivers and lakes, seas and oceans, lost their tolerance to untreated waste products. Even the bio-system of the atmosphere, which had been assumed to be as vast and adaptable as space itself, was shown to have limited tolerance to gaseous or dust emissions. And so there developed a dramatic concern for the environment, ecology and conservation, and demands, from those with a healthy positive balance in their consumption accounts, for zero or negative growth. Were this policy to be followed in the absence of population stabilisation, the rise of the mediocracy would give way to the rise of the paupocracy.

Technology has a number of philosophical and social consequences that are less in the news. Many people are bemused by its exponential growth. Like it or loathe it – and it is now fashionable in the West to loathe it – they are inclined to believe that its growth parallels that of science and inventions. If this assumption were challenged they would point to the number of science graduates, research institutes and registered patents. It is another case of the equation of quality and quantity, to be expected in a world that is experiencing the decline and fall of the intellectual and the problem of bigness without comment, perhaps without comprehension.

One does not need to recognise a total picture to be familiar with some of its pigments. What is happening in technology can be understood without reference to all the concepts that relate to the rise of the mediocracy. If the rise of technology crested a wave of rising science and inventiveness, it might of course be doubted whether there were really a decline and fall of the intellectual or a rise of the mediocracy. The absence of this wave, on the other hand, depends to some extent on the intellectual's fate in society but not on that alone. Moreover, in modern society the scientist is not necessarily an 'intellectual'. Whatever the genetic requirements of either may be, their training is different and their output non-comparable. Intellectualism is either ignored or despised; science either admired or disliked. Even if the scientist and the intellectual are regarded as genetically similar, and if it is agreed that aspirants can be recognised by IQ tests or examination passes, science – or at any rate the physical sciences – seems to be at a disadvantage in acquiring brainpower. For reasons largely beyond its control and to be blamed on commercial interests or a failure of political nerve, from science have emerged the Bomb and the intercontinental ballistic missile, chemical pollution and noise pollution. For all the faults of pre-scientific society, many observers feel 'repose and quiet has been drowned by a ceaseless roar on earth and in the sky' and a 'sense of peace and security . . . in the course of this century has been taken from us'.[1] To blame these developments on scientists may be unjustified, but it has happened. The result is that in many secondary schools throughout the world – where political pressures do not impinge directly on Academe – the most sensitive and able students are turning from the sciences to the arts. By an academic yardstick, therefore, science should be a relative sufferer whatever the overall fate of education or the intellectual. That this yardstick is inadequate may be deduced

[1] Harold Macmillan, *At the End of the Day, 1961–1963*, London and Basingstoke, 1973, pp. 521 and 522.

from equally dismal performances in the arts. So one may look beyond personnel to basic problems of science and technology.

As similar forecasts in the past have been invalidated by events, it is undoubtedly reckless to assert that we are already knocking at the frontiers of basic knowledge. Yet recklessness is sometimes warranted. It is surely demonstrated scientifically – whatever people may choose to believe by faith or hunch – that the universe is essentially mechanistic and that 'laws' of psychology, biology and astronomy are ultimately derived from the laws of physics and chemistry. Evolutionary studies and genetic maps, relativity studies and radiation physics, quantum mechanics and atomic models have demonstrated the interrelationship of man and the universe in its broad pattern. Attempts to blow up and penetrate this pattern to its innermost secrets are already pushing against critical frontiers: complexity of instrumentation, where artifacts get confounded with nature and speculative induction is replacing simple inference; belated recognition that man is both observer and observed and that a part of nature cannot comprehend the whole; belated recognition that empiricism cannot give definitive answers to 'original' questions concerning the universe and life. Perhaps these facts are not fully recognised today. Only a few years ago in certain countries philosophy was dominated by the mediocrats of logical positivism. By asserting that the only meaningful propositions were tautological or empirical, whereby they hoped to disentangle science from superstition, they reached the position of implying that in matters like cosmogony or revealed religion, where neither observation nor experimentation was possible, there was really nothing to choose between rational reconstruction and irrational speculation. This mystical legacy has been repudiated by some academic beneficiaries, but it has probably been inherited by more than Jesus freaks and Hindu *gurus*. Be that as it may, while the scientific map of the universe is generally acknowledged, at least by scientists, in broad outline, the details of its capes and bays, reefs and sandbanks have never been in greater dispute and look decreasingly capable of resolution.

Non-scientists may feel instinctively that this is a problem for pure scientists and that they have enough worries of their own. Whatever may be the fate of science, they mutter, the rise of technology demonstrates the advance of applied science. Certainly there are areas, like air transport, where this seems to be true – and, save for those who live near airports, the social cost of fossil fuel depletion, vapour and noise pollution may still be less than the social benefit of increased speed and safety. At all events, heavier-than-air machines, from biplanes to luniks, are the peculiar triumph of the twentieth century. When one looks at the other technological marvels of our age, however, one finds that most of them were invented, or discovered, in the nineteenth century: dynamo, turbine, railway, electric tram, internal combustion engine, bicycle, pneumatic tyre, telegraph, telephone, radio, plastics, synthetic fibres, aniline dyes, skyscraper, steel, tractor, typewriter, gramophone, camera, cinema, stethoscope, X-rays, immunisation, pasteurisation, zip fastener, safety pin, safety match, electric light, electric iron, hot-plate, vacuum cleaner, refrigerator, washing machine, spin-dryer and dishwasher. One has to chase further back into history to trace the origins of gaslight, powered spinning, sewing and weaving machines, submarine, telescope, barometer, steam engine, microscope, thermometer, printing press, gunpowder and metallurgy. Despite prefabrication, new materials and the electronic revolution, the basic design of houses has not changed in hundreds of years, and the main differences between contemporary and bygone dwellings are that today windows and doors are less likely to function and the life expectancy is considerably reduced. Excluding television, there is probably no significant item in personal or domestic use in the twentieth century whose prototype was not invented in preceding centuries. And, apart from new methods of power generation and transport – which are of primary concern to affluent individuals in affluent countries – the twentieth century cannot in the non-personal and non-domestic fields claim credit for much save weapons development. Seen in this perspective, technology need not wonder at its bad name. But how is it possible to speak of a rise of technology?

The truth is that technology, both beneficent and threatening, is derivative and like other derivative things is capable of multiple variations on the original. Nineteenth-century inventions grew out of basic discoveries in the exploration of matter and energy in the eighteenth century. Twentieth-century technology has grown out of the basic inventions of the nineteenth century. Every industrial process is the operation of complex variables, each one of which can be changed in turn under controlled experimental conditions. Under working conditions any change in one variable is likely to lead to changes in the rest, requiring new materials and new processes. The modern industrial plant incorporates semi-autonomous research and development units which pursue their own investigations with little thought of the original technology or product that brought the plant into being. If a promising new process turns up by the logic of experimentation, the logic of satisfying an established market is abandoned and the company starts manufacturing products related to its new processes rather than to its old products. Thus change feeds on change. Technology is becoming another outlet for neophilia.

Other developments have affected the type of person likely to engage in science or technology. The back-shed inventor has suffered in the general decline of the intellectual and the self-employed. If it is true that most basic discoveries calling for inspired insights have already been made, he is most unlikely to make one now. If he seeks to develop a basic process he is most unlikely to be able to meet the capital costs involved. However successful he may be at invention, he is faced with growing problems of patent law complexity, industrial espionage, huge production costs and the risk of being bought out to kill rather than nourish the discovery. It would be optimistic to think he could ever amass enough capital to set up an operation like Edison's which would place a great apparatus of men and machinery at his entrepreneurial fingertips. The result is that most research today is done in laboratories owned by governments or private corporations, both influenced by the rise of bureaucracy and the philias, and modified by, respectively, political and commercial pressures. Governments and company directors are equally aware that research has its fashions and development its trends, and know that new variations on an old theme are, on the whole, more respectable and more profitable than new themes. Tiny operations are indefinitely repeated, changing this parameter or that or making no conscious change at all, in the hope that chance will throw up a new product or a new process. Priorities and promotions are determined by committees and contracted by lawyers, constrained by accountants and conveyed by publicists. In smaller academic establishments the nominal head of a research institute may wield personal power, but academic politics and publishers' deadlines moderate creativity. In replacing the lone wolf of science by the hunting pack of production engineering, technology has brought deflation to individualists and elation to mediocrats.

While providing jobs for the mediocracy, which has a special flair for filling places where talent might once have been expected, technology has exercised debilitating influence over us all. With electric light it has brought intellectual darkness. It has cluttered up our lives with radios and television sets, gramophones and cassette recorders, motor-cars, and motor-boats – or a lusting after them. It has filled our homes with gadgetry of innumerable brands and models, in the service of which we continually seek spare parts and maintenance, convertible attachments and compatible accessories. It has turned our places of work and recreation – even of worship, if in desperation we have turned to religion – into alien, continually changing environments, where everything is different and little is improved. But it has achieved its purpose in providing a brave new world for the mediocracy.

CHAPTER NINE

Population Explosion

'Resource management is frequently discussed without reference to the population explosion ... the survival of the unfittest. .... The population explosion is differentially among the poorest, most diseased, dullest and most insensitive members of the species.'

The explosion of technology has distinguished itself by two other explosions: thermonuclear and population. While it threatens the extinction of all -cracies, the Bomb showers a fallout of anxiety neurosis which can only fertilise the mediocracy. It fortifies the midnight prompting that all life is evanescent, nothing is finally important. The radical chic have not been slow to dilate on the dangers of nuclear explosion to generations alive or yet to be born. But the population explosion is another thing, not to be agonised over. True, some media mediocrats have found a new goldmine shovelling out the Pill to glossy journals that would, a decade ago, have relegated contraception to the brothel, but the full implications of a plague of people and effective antibiotic treatment are carefully avoided. Other media mediocrats, usually of Roman Catholic persuasion, eschew the Pill and deny the population explosion. If God-given medical technology has brought us more people, God-given food technology will allow us to feed them: so the argument runs. Or, they say, forgetting that affluence brings better medical services and so raises life expectancy, as people become more affluent they tend to have smaller families.

This is not the place to argue that a population which is doubling every generation or so is in fact exploding. Neither need

we go to the other extreme and assert the situation is so out of
hand that if everyone declared for contraception tomorrow
disaster would still overtake us by the end of the century.
Dramatic forecasts of doom are usually related to consumption
of energy and strategic metals and overlook a number of facts:
there are immense known 'uneconomic' deposits, which are uneconomic because the materials are not yet so scarce as to raise
their price to economic levels; with strenuous exploration, known
deposits would almost certainly multiply; there is virtually unlimited energy potential in the sun; recycling of scarce resources is
only in its infancy, again because they are not yet scarce enough
to make it profitable. Does this then mean that the population
explosion is unimportant? Not at all. Squandering of finite
resources is not to be ignored because it may have been
exaggerated. Moreover, resource management is frequently discussed without reference to the population explosion, whose
ripples are becoming billows without even the barrier of wringing
hands.

Producing adequate food for the world's millions is one of the
more intractable problems facing technology. Despite new strains
of grain, insecticides in fields and antibiotics in food animals
(which are bringing their own problems), fish farming, factory
farming (which is morally disturbing) and artificial fertilisers,
agriculture and animal husbandry are not yet feeding the world's
current population adequately. What is technically edible is not
necessarily eaten and even the hungry may not rush to a dinner
of algae, artichokes and foul-smelling fish-meal. Though 'starving' people on the Malthusian pattern are the subject of most
reportage of the Third World – limited as reports are – 'hungry'
is a more accurate description for most. For everyone who dies,
many remain alive undernourished or malnourished; and though
their potency or fertility may be reduced, they are not childless.

In many areas there are scarcer things than food. Water is the
most vital of them. Where there is enough to drink there may not
be enough for irrigation, effluent disposal, sewerage or hygiene.
Sinking wells, seeding clouds and evaporating saline have been
aided by technology, but the growth in water supply has not
matched either the rise in population or rising expectations. Land
is another resource of finite dimensions and potentialities. The
main reason why food production has slowed down is that we are
running out of fertile land. Arable acres are yearly swallowed up
in expanding cities, reservoirs, motorways and other artifacts of

civilisation. In the first industrial revolution exploration and forest clearing opened up new agricultural land, but there is little of the world left to explore and forests are needed for cellulose products. Agricultural expansion is now occurring in marshes and heathland, tundra and other 'virgin' lands whose promise is brighter than their performance. In an ecstasy of desperation, scientists are now talking of yet more alien, arid, inaccessible and inhospitable regions: on the moon and other planets, or even other solar systems – surely the wildest colonisation proposals ever made by scientific mediocrats. Alternatively, they talk chattily of subterranean or submarine cities as if human intelligence and sensitivity had sunk so low that the 'decline and fall of the intellectual' should be called the 'rise and triumph of congenital idiots'. Even more cheerful are those Roman Catholic economists who describe how many people the earth's surface will support standing shoulder to shoulder.

To pass on from basic requirements of sustenance and shelter, we see that the population explosion is threatening requirements technology does not pretend to satisfy: or, rather, used not to pretend to satisfy till the rise of pharmacophilia. These are areas of natural beauty, pockets of wild life, space to be alone in – all the things that satisfy the human species' exceptional demand for biological living space and ecological balance. If zoo studies point the hostility and aggression that accompany confinement of less sensitive animals, how much greater is man's response to claustrophobia. Sociological studies have already shown that crime, delinquency, vandalism, drugtaking and prostitution are higher in big cities than in towns, villages and the countryside, where population densities are lower. And, despite decentralisation policies throughout the world, mechanisation of primary industries and the rise of service industries are accelerating the drift to the cities, whose social problems are self-perpetuating. With the population explosion fortifying this drift, their social problems are self-accelerating. In this climate a growing proportion of the world's growing population is fated to eke out existence.

In some lucky countries *per capita* consumption of resources may for a while continue to rise. In that case, individuals will mature sexually earlier, grow taller and live longer than their ancestors, but there is no evidence, on past experience, that they will grow in intelligence or wisdom to cope with increasing challenges. Indeed, there is every reason to expect a statistical decline. This is a picture likely to be reproduced in more lurid colours throughout the world. For the population explosion of the human species is not, as in other species, a 'survival of the fittest' or at least a proliferation of the biological norm. In fact, it would not be an exaggeration to call it the survival of the unfittest.

The very expression 'population explosion' suggests forces that, however they arise, are impersonal in their expansion. This is, however, far from the case. Though certain social conditions impinge equally on all sections of the community, others operate preferentially. Above all, population trends are the result of innumerable individual decisions that are as diverse as those who make them. Yet they band together to create macroscopic patterns.

In psychological terms a population explosion is a contraceptive collapse. For one reason or another, people are proving more fecund than population stabilisation demands. If they do not oppose contraception, they are not its loyal followers. There are many possible motivations. They may be ignorant of the benefit or the practice of effective contraception. Coming from poor countries with inadequate medical or welfare services they may choose to have large families to increase the chance of raising children as an insurance policy for their old age. They may be constrained by religious beliefs to oppose contraception as a human presumption or to avoid reliable means of achieving it. Either because religious beliefs of this sort – e.g. Roman Catholicism, Islam or Hinduism – are a response to endemic poverty or because their socio-economic teachings predispose towards it, they tend to flourish in poor countries. Nationalist or racialist views may also dictate opposition to contraception, which is deemed to be 'ethnic suicide'. Again, such views tend to flourish in poor or primitive communities. In most countries, whatever their background, those who are least likely to worry about contraception or the fate of the world are, by and large, the most thoughtless, feckless, reckless, unintelligent or depressed members of society. Consequently, the population explosion is more than a nondescript plague of people. At a time when it is fashionable to talk much of 'man in the saddle' directing the course of evolution and of 'genetic engineering' as the harness he uses, it is ironic that the population explosion is differentially among the poorest, most diseased, dullest and most insensitive members of the species. This is more than just a suspect value-judgement of the 'natural' population increase. Partly for kindly humanitarian reasons, however misplaced, but often through religious pressures or medical experimentation, in the richer countries there is an 'unnatural' increase of growing and disturbing proportions. This consists of neonatal 'monsters' and geriatric 'vegetables' who would not have survived in a state of nature but are bullied and badgered into metabolism (one can hardly call it 'life') by batteries of gadgets and crucibles of chemicals. Through no fault of their own they are consuming a disproportionate share of specialist skills of every sort. Yet they remain, as individuals, financially disadvantaged, and if they are capable of thought at all eke out their existence in understandable discontentment. If they are fertile there are desultory efforts to persuade – even to trick – them not to procreate, but these attempts are denounced as a monstrous attack on human freedom and dignity. So society struggles on with proportionally fewer arms feeding and caring for proportionally more mouths, occasionally stopping to ask querulously why we never seem to clear the slums, abolish poverty or build enough schools and hospitals. As media mediocrats inveigh against eugenics, euthanasia, élitism and 'social Darwinism' – all of which are ingeniously equated with Hitler's gas chambers[1] – society is increasingly anti-eugenic, hostile to even voluntary euthanasia, opposed to all élites save the mediocracy and dedicated to 'social Rousseauanism'.

In the short term, therefore, we live in a world of perpetual crisis and sense of crisis, forever chasing the temporary and the palliative at the expense of the permanent and the curative. The result is mediocrity and the rise of the mediocracy. If present trends continue into the long term, we may exchange mediocrity for decrepitude and the mediocracy for the paupocracy.

[1] Of doubtful historicity. See Paul Rassinier, *Le Mensonge d'Ulysse*, Paris, 1949, and *Le drame des Juifs européens*, Paris, 1964.

CHAPTER TEN

Problem of Bigness

'While "participation" flourishes as a vogue, if not a cant, term, bigness is making effective participation in government increasingly difficult. . . . The problem of bigness has raised impassable cybernetic barriers to the free flow of information and personal contacts.'

A few years ago it was possible – so possible that it happened – to lecture to a radical-chic audience in one of the world's most intellectual suburbs on 'The Problem of Bigness' to universal disapproval. It could be assumed in advance that the subject was neither radical nor chic, but the lecturer thought it would be deemed intellectually respectable. To the great bulk of the audience, however, it turned out to be neither respectable nor comprehensible. It is doubtful if the response would be very different today, save that one item in the thesis – the population explosion – might sound familiar enough to be academically reputable.

In political terms the population explosion has had a number of consequences. Perhaps they are not as important as the biological and social consequences outlined in the previous chapter, but they are far from negligible. Coupled with the rise of democracy and the collapse of systems and authority, population increase has contributed to both centripetal and centrifugal forces inside every political unit. It is tending to make some nation-states very large indeed while boosting tensions within them leading to separatist movements. Together with colonial emancipation, these movements, largely based on religious or racial differences, are increasing quite dramatically the number of independent states recognised by the United Nations. This dual phenomenon of bigger nations and more nations has caused diverse problems. Apart from their connection with bigness they are united by their mothering of the mediocracy.

While 'participation' flourishes as a vogue, if not a cant, term, bigness is making effective participation in government increasingly difficult. The rise of technology and bureaucracy and other invincible social forces are tending to augment the powers of central, as distinct from provincial or local, government unless or until separatist forces by military means achieve fragmentation. Where these giant states remain united, their national assemblies are experiencing one or other – or usually both together – of the following trends: with the creation of new constituencies they are composed of more members; each constituency is growing larger. Sometimes it is impossible for national debating chambers to seat all their members at any one time, while, notwithstanding electronic gadgetry, they are losing their deliberative atmosphere and becoming more like market halls or indoor circuses. Political grandstanding enjoys architectural support. Not that debates matter very much in a situation where no one is influenced by them and all decisions are taken in caucus rooms or whips' offices before each debate begins. In the exercise of other parliamentary business, bigness of membership brings the same cybernetic problems as other large systems experience. Outside Parliament the bigness of constituencies sets up a train of events. It becomes more difficult for candidates or members to woo or serve electors individually. In so far as they are reached at all it is by the mass media, and the majority of constituents would not recognise their local member if they bumped into him in the street. The solemn debate over whether Members of Parliament are representatives or delegates, with an undefined or specific brief, becomes farcical when the bulk of their constituents feel no relationship with them at all. As electorates become bigger they tend to lose local colour and idiosyncrasies, community identity and community involvement, particular needs and particular desires in representation. Faced with nations composed of such constituencies, political parties are therefore driven to selecting similar candidates – similar throughout the country and especially similar to their opposite number in each electorate. Whether such candidates are, as individuals, mediocrities, they are certainly cogs in a mediocratic machine.

What has happened in politics has happened in other fields:

business, education, bureaucracy, law, medicine. *Laissez-faire* capitalism has become monopoly capitalism, companies have merged into corporations and national corporations into multi-national corporations. Schools, colleges and universities are growing ever larger and more impersonal and the only reason why it is inappropriate to speak of them as academic factories is that they usually enjoy lower standards of hygiene, health and safety regulations. As populations grow and government involvement grows, new departments are created. To ensure the status of each, higher-grade officers and a suitable number of subordinates are appointed whatever the function of the United Nations commission, national department, branch or section involved. As populations and crime expand, police forces have lost the 'man on the beat' who knew his locality intimately in favour of the mobile squad car and impersonal team. At the punitive end of law enforcement courts have become court complexes, hearings are so delayed that witnesses have forgotten their testimony by the time they are called, and individual magistrates and judges are so out of contact they find it impossible to reach anything approaching uniformity of sentencing. As populations increase in size and mobility, the 'family doctor', who knew the antecedents and social circumstances of his patients intimately and was thus likely to detect hereditary diseases and psychosomatic conditions, has become, at best, the individual doctor who knows his patient as a cypher with a case history or, at worst, a machine that responds to every input of signs and symptoms with a scribbled prescription and a bill or health service chit. Patients need not interpret this response as a personal slight, since the modern doctor is likely to be as out of touch with his profession as he is with them. In every case, the problem of bigness has raised impassable cybernetic barriers to the free flow of information and personal contacts. This is one modern problem that is, in certain areas, recognised. Co-ordinators, communicators and consultants flourish like the green bay tree. Within governmental or private complexes they not infrequently form units that are so large they have their own internal cybernetic problems. Public relations experts are so numerous they scarcely manage to 'relate' to one another, let alone to the public, which is seen as an alien irrelevance. In every field of endeavour more energy is consumed discovering how to communicate than what to communicate; or, more accurately, asking how to communicate than what to communicate.

Even more than the growth of people and institutions, the 'information explosion' has produced this cybernetic *impasse*. While his full potentialities may seldom be realised, the individual has very finite capacities for comprehension, retention and, above all, productive use of knowledge. Sophisticated computerised information collection, storage and retrieval systems have disguised this basic fact. Programming and co-ordinating the output of computers is still a task for individual technocrats. Much more could probably be done by computers themselves, but they lack a sympathetic political climate to be entrusted with this job and much of what they do already is simply filed away and forgotten. Instead of dictating they talk to us, or rather to cyberneticians. The professional communicators give no greater indication of omniscience than any other professional group and have indeed created a jargon more impenetrable to the layman than many non-communicating cliques.

The systematisation of knowledge has involved the compartmentalisation of knowledge. It has enabled branches of learning to be given labels and curators – experts dedicated to their preservation, growth and further subdivision. As nature is a unity and man a psychosomatic continuum, these divisions are entirely artificial. For a time they enable problems to be isolated and studied under controlled conditions, but as they become increasingly arbitrary and autonomous they create a greater problem of disunity and fragmented vision. As each field of study reaches the critical point where further subdivision is impossible, vision effectively disappears altogether. We are left with a multitude of specialist studies conducted by innumerable small pedants unable to communicate effectively either with the general public or with one another. Within the fortresses of their several disciplines, protected by impenetrable language and professional closed shops, they flourish immune from criticism because they are beyond the reach of comprehension. The world which the Augustans and the Victorians were making accessible has become inaccessible again and people are returning to religion or striking out after newer and sometimes stranger cults in an effort to find holism for the universe and themselves. In the place of the polymath have come the charlatan and the mediocrat. One is happy giving silly answers to every question, the other giving every answer to silly questions.

Meanwhile the 'intelligentsia' – politicians, media men, reviewers and other groups that lay claim to an Olympian overview – are overwhelmed in their desire to be 'well-informed'. They cannot personally cultivate every offshoot of learning, so they take short cuts round the tree of knowledge. Sometimes they master, or think they master, one or two disciplines, then extrapolate their findings, or purported findings, into the whole world of experience, where specialist conclusions may be invalid. Sometimes they settle for being the echo of other people's ideas, but which people and what ideas? So they rush to abstracts of learned papers, then abstracts of abstracts, then abstracts of abstracts of abstracts. They begin as culture vultures and end as parasites in the feathers of vultures. Generally they avoid abstracts altogether and chase more colourful presentations in glossy magazines or popularising paperbacks. As these are mostly written by people like themselves, the presentation is invariably superficial and often inaccurate. And as there is no Renaissance mandarin to offer guidance for their overall reading list, the magazines or paperbacks, produced in ever more bewildering abundance, that they read are matters of pure fortuity. In their assessments of creative artists they make the same arbitrary 'choices' – or, rather, cling to the names that are trendy and the opinions that media mediocrats pass on. It has always been difficult for the layman to apply artistic criteria to creative output and establish a hierarchy of excellence. Today the task is virtually impossible. Though each creative artist is tending to produce less work – in line with general trends in productivity – the number of artists, dead and living, is multiplying hourly and confounding connoisseurs with the problem of bigness, while the collapse of systems has made even *cognoscenti* hesitate to apply artistic criteria to anyone or anything. In such circumstances 'name dropping' has passed from an affectation to a necessity.

A similar problem of bigness faces the creative artist himself. Unless he is a member of the growing band of *aficionados* of 'feeling', for whom art has no past, no canons and no future but fructifies in an eternal now, he will seek to dig down to the roots of his craft before climbing to its treetops. But below each succeeding generation these roots are buried ever deeper in a topsoil of time and convoluted more crazily by indiscriminate fertilisation. The past has a lengthening evolution and the present is so fragmented into 'schools' and trends that it is difficult to see how – or if – it is developing. If the artist abandons, as well he may, the spirit of 'art' for the stuff of life, he runs into further problems. Life is so complex, its ingredients so numerous, its influences so diverse. Despite the 'global village' of television, the artist's background of knowledge and experience is increasingly idiosyncratic, rootless, classless and unrelated to that of other artists from which he used to derive sustenance, inspiration and a yardstick to measure his own impressions and achievements. Because of the global village of television the artist is bombarded from his earliest years with a diversity of cultures ancient and modern, reconstructed or filmed live, so that he has no sense of personal cultural heritage, absorbs more than he can assimilate and assimilates more than he can channel into art. Our cultural scene has become a wilderness overgrown by stunted shrubs. It is not surprising that the twentieth century will be remembered – if it is remembered at all – for the existentialist novel and abstract art. Where there are no accepted measures of excellence, excellence is liable to trickle away before the satisfied eye of a mediocracy that has no use for it. People of universal merit are hard to recognise and shunned if they are.

While it has contributed impressively to the rise of mediocrities the problem of bigness disturbs them too. Indeed, having few inner resources and less imagination, though not without powers of observation, mediocrities are more likely than most to experience psychological difficulty 'relating' to vast, daunting architecture and vast impersonal institutions and communities. The overall advantage of a caste is, however, more important to its members than is their personal inconvenience, and mediocrities may take comfort from the unrestricted rise of the mediocracy.

CHAPTER ELEVEN

Rise of Bureaucracy

'If the system stands to lose more by action than inaction, each bureaucrat inclined to new initiatives must weigh the substantial personal cost of failure against the modest personal advantage of success. . . . Bureaucracy has become a great oak that attracts every sort of social ivy . . . a cornucopia of goodies that somebody else is paying for.'

The problem of bigness has led to the rise of bureaucracy. With the growing size of institutions it has become impossible to have a direct relationship between employer and employee, governor and governed, producer and consumer. Workers rarely meet, or even see, all the directors of their operating company, much less the directors of its (possibly overseas) holding company or share-holders scattered round the world. For their part, shareholders have little effective control over the actions of directors, who arrive at annual general meetings with more voting proxies than frank answers, and little knowledge of the company's operations. The French Revolution largely took place because citizens were disturbed by the corruption, size and remoteness of the King's Civil Service. Under democratic auspices the Civil Service may be less corrupt but it is just as remote and infinitely bigger. Protocol and security make it more, rather than less, difficult today for the ordinary person to approach the executive directly, while democratic elections unseat popular representatives so frequently that it is necessary to have a strong bureaucracy to ensure stability and continuity. In modern commerce, barter has virtually disappeared before the onrush of processing, whole-saling and retailing operations, mediated by credit and other financial arrangements, in bringing a growing diversity of pro-

ducts to urbanised consumers increasingly remote from and
ignorant of the primary producer. Schools have grown so big that
headteachers rarely teach, hospitals so big that medical super-
intendents rarely see patients. In every field the chain of
command has become so attenuated that there has arisen a class
of intermediaries to regulate administration, feedback and co-
ordination.

Other bureaucratic tendencies have arisen from the rise of
democracy and the problem of bigness. Though the nineteenth-
century creed of individualism reversed the tendency for a while,
democracy has roused expectations of equal access, as of right, to
basic services and amenities. If these are to be guaranteed, the
State must guarantee them. Personal circumstances and initiative
cannot be relied on, since these may, hypothetically, vanish at
any time through misfortune. It is ironic that in modern times it
is largely the Left that has complained of the rise of bureaucracy
since Leftist demands for more State education, medicine, welfare, control over industry and international relations are largely
responsible for this phenomenon. For, whatever other attractions
'utopian' socialist communities may offer, it is State bureaucracy
which dispenses the social and other sophisticated services
demanded by modern dependent man. With the knowledge
explosion and growth of specialisation these demands are
expanding. It is felt that as supplies of possible goods and
services grow there is more the State can supply; and such is the
momentum of expectations, the more the State can supply, the
more the State should supply. Just as within each discipline
intermediaries are needed between individuals and groups
formerly in direct contact, so in the community at large they link
up disciplines to form an ordered whole and confer on each some
measure of public accountability. Once public expenditure was
met from the Sovereign's Privy Purse, augmented where needed
by special levies of men and money to fight foreign or civil wars.
Outside 'public works' (royal palaces, for example) such expenditure was minimal and – despite misconceptions to the contrary –
direct public control was also minimal. The Church was
entrusted with sacred building, disciplining the clergy and
administering whatever educational, medical or charitable institutions there might be. Craftsmen were regulated by their guilds
and merchants by their corporations. Citizens relied on themselves or their servants for personal protection. Apart from the

Sovereign's bodyguard, soldiers were demobilised in peacetime. Today the State has taken over, or oversees, all these functions, and bureaucracy is its instrument. Marxists say it will wither away. Anarchists and voices from the 'alternative society' want to abolish it. But it is more established than motherhood. Though in its current guise it is relatively modern, its origins can be traced back to the beginning of history, when the invention of writing made it possible to record and easier to regulate social events. 'The goose quill put an end to talk. It abolished mystery; it gave architecture and towns; it brought roads and armies, bureaucracy.'[1]

The rise of bureacracy has brought many consequences for man and society. In a societal context it has advanced classification tendencies furthered by science throughout the physical world. This has induced a love of the readily classifiable and distrust of the maverick, the great original that bounds over natural and artificial boundaries. By contrast, mediocrity fits snugly in its humdrum place. Classification is linked with stratification, the creation of a complex hierarchy split into countless – but not nameless – divisions and grades each with subtle differentials. Deference is not to knowledge, experience or ability but to higher rungs in the bureaucratic ladder. Since dismissal is extremely difficult, these rungs may well be occupied by people who make up in seniority or conviviality (and often in religion, background, schooling or fraternity) what they lack in integrity or ability. Above all, there is a high premium on conformity, brought about by many pressures.

In the 'reformed' Civil Service of one liberal democracy, which happens to be the United Kingdom but could be almost anywhere else:

> No longer were officials dependent for the highest prizes in their careers on their success within their Departments, as was the case when these were almost independent in their policy of promotion, which encouraged a spirit of reform. Constructive thinking became a dangerous quality. It was 'reputation for solid commonsense', i.e. the favour of a small Treasury clique, which became decisive. The fact that Civil Servants are supposed to be permanent has, far from promoting detailed

[1] Marshall McLuhan, *The Medium is the Massage*, New York, 1967, p. 48.

and free thought, resulted in a depressing conformity – very different from earlier periods.[1]

As the bureaucracy gains more effective power *vis-à-vis* its political masters, so it becomes more important in a democracy to pretend otherwise. Fortified by the growing tendency of political parties themselves to cultivate the 'middle ground', this pretence in practice means that the bureaucracy usually avoids initiating any new proposals of its own and warns incoming ministries of the possible hazards attached to any brave new schemes they may have. Life is easier, it says, if everyone follows the mixture as before, modified only by the findings of the latest statistics. Since these are themselves a reflection of the past, and not always of the immediate past, they may give a totally mis-leading picture of current activities in the world at large, which is also aware of statistical trends and – apparently unknown to the bureaucracy – has already taken remedial action. This is a likely explanation of the disastrous advice that, especially in times of radical change, governments get from their Treasuries; so that they inflate the economy when they ought to deflate and deflate when they ought to inflate. It is one thing to escape the scourge of neophilia and to promote political, social and moral stability, as the bureaucracy does. It is another to react sluggishly on practical issues when prompt action is required, or to be so out of phase with cyclical patterns that the response is opposite to what is needed.

If the philosophy of bureaucratic functioning has caused dis-quiet, recruitment procedures have not allayed it. In many countries twentieth-century evolution 'formally established the superiority of those recruits to the Civil Service who had no professional or technical qualifications'.[2] This might have been a welcome return to the tradition of the Renaissance man bringing a masterly overview to the work of innumerable experts, were other factors not at work. So complex are today's specialities that some professional or technical knowledge is necessary to assess them, or even to understand them. This can be acquired as well in a work setting as in an academic setting – probably better – but it demands job continuity. It has, however, become fashion-able to move individuals around from section to section, branch

[1] Thomas Balogh, 'The Apotheosis of the Dilettante', in *The Establishment*, p. 88.
[2] Ibid., p. 88.

D

to branch, department to department so rapidly that they never have time to learn the fundamentals of those operations their department is called on to organise, whether it be taxation law, town planning or technological development. The best they can hope for is mastery of the basic skills of 'administration' – an imposing polysyllable which may mean little more than office routine. Imperfectly understanding the professional and technical requirements of their department, they are unlikely to be rash enough to suggest innovation. The caution of unfamiliarity fortifies a devotion to established procedures at the individual level matching that of bureaucracy as a whole. For if the system stands to lose more by action than inaction, each bureaucrat inclined to new initiatives must weigh the substantial personal cost of failure against the modest personal advantage of success. If his innovation fails – perhaps through the timidity of colleagues rather than basic deficiency – while he is unlikely to be sacked he will be disowned by superiors, shunned by the minister and retarded in or barred from promotion by an indelible memo in his personal file. If his innovation succeeds, the credit will probably go to superiors or to the minister, he will gain no pecuniary reward and a favourable memo will count little in promotion against the more pressing demands of seniority, 'influence' and such extraneous factors as affect recruitment. Clearly there are occasions when it is intelligent to appear unintelligent and in special circumstances a team of geniuses can form a mediocracy.

There is, however, no reason to believe that bureaucracy is recruiting either geniuses or Renaissance men. Where there are entrance exams, 'the qualifying examination is too weak to exclude feeble intellects'. Where there is psychological testing, 'the test itself ... seems to favour the grasshopper mind and the exhibitionist'. In some bureaucracies, the academic background of recruits shows a 'predominance of classics and mathematics' – in other words, special devotion to a world which is dead or a world which is idealised. This 'necessarily encourages acceptance of precedents, however ill-fitting, and a refusal, because of incapacity, to think out problems afresh'.[1]

At the upper echelons of the Civil Service can be found 'effective power without responsibility, the complete freedom from all criticism, and last but not least, the attainment of higher

[1] Ibid., p. 92.

salaries than their Ministerial chiefs'.[1] It is a position not altogether dissimilar to that of company managers in relation to shareholders, 'middlemen' in relation to primary producers, or agents in relation to the people they represent. But this is because bureaucracy has passed beyond the Civil Service to infiltrate other aspects of life, where it has a similar *modus operandi*, attracts the same sort of people and has the same social consequences. In special fields these consequences are confined. Nationally they can be more serious.

> The disastrous effects of the Treasury's and the Bank of England's financial policy during the inter-war period are no longer questioned. They left Britain economically weaker and its population shocked by the traumatic experience of mass-unemployment. The impact of the Treasury during the Second War was almost fatal. At its beginning the successful opposition of the Treasury and the Bank of England against a firm control of foreign payments cost the country hundreds of millions in gold.... Attempts have been made, by the indefatigable penmen of the bureaucracy, to defend the drift towards conformity and the measures causing it as an inevitable requirement of living in a new and dangerous age. So far as Britain is concerned there can be no doubt that the consequential deadening effect which eliminates originality has resulted in a relative decline in Britain's strength and influence.[2]

This decline might have been greater had similar influences not been operating in other countries, where it is not unknown to find more people administering than being administered.

Apart from its impact on the nation as a whole, the bureaucracy has a growing influence on individuals, however indigent or affluent they may be. Form-filling has become a universal way of life; if the subject is illiterate, scribes are provided. Documentation has invaded privacy and the slightest signs of nonconformity in youth are reported, computerised and filed away in data banks – or soon will be. All aspects of our life are taken care of – at a price, and a growing one. Taxes, contributions and premiums to protect against possible insecurity in the future are so onerous that we experience certain insecurity in the present. In

[1] Ibid., p. 98.
[2] Ibid., pp. 105 and 110.

both socialist and non-socialist countries there is a

> persistent notion that the State can somehow act as the comptroller of private demand and the creator of industrial capacity. The main consequence of this has been to give the State the power to destroy private savings.... But I want to see the central bank separated again from government; I want to see State borrowing powers limited as they once were: I want to see taxation confined to what is required to meet the legitimate needs of the State and not used to manipulate society. I think we should think first of looking after our own welfare and not expect the community to do it automatically for us.[1]

Bureaucracy has become a great oak that attracts every sort of social ivy. While free-living plants are, often through no fault of their own, uprooted and die in proud poverty, the sappy limbs of bureaucracy are festooned with parasites: businessmen with constant clamour for subsidies, tariff protection, and tax deductions (if they have not managed to channel all their earnings through tax havens, where the issue does not arise); certain trades unions on annual (or more frequent) strike for higher wages while their 'dependants' live on social security; hippies who accept welfare benefits without interrupting their denunciations of society long enough to say 'thank you'; and a variety of professional bruised reeds who have capitalised their deprivations. To all of these groups bureaucracy is a cornucopia of goodies that somebody else is paying for. Yet media mediocrats talk of 'free medicine', 'free education' or 'free milk' as if they are, in every sense, free.

Though the decline and fall of the intellectual and the hapless state of the arts themselves have made other factors of limited importance, bureaucracy has had a profound impact on creative artists. It has become a prime source of artistic patronage. Donors and connoisseurs have yielded to boards and committees. Mediocratic judgements have taken over from personal assessments, which might have been capricious but were at least colourful. Moreover, an enlightened bureaucracy – wherever it exists – has the quality of a reputable charity: a substantial part of the money collected goes to administration and promotion, not to the advertised recipients. This operational wastage is justified on the grounds that bureaucracy seeks and finds deserving artists

[1] Paul Einzig, 'Immoral Inflation', in *New Humanist*, February 1974.

who would not otherwise gain support. Why creative *Heidenrösleins* too shy to hunt out private patrons (if they existed) should pluck up courage to apply for bureaucratic grants is not explained. Neither is it at all clear how the towering, and perhaps prickly, genius whose nonconformism might offend individual benefactors is likely to appeal more to a cultural committee. All one deduces from the broad scope of bureaucratic patronage round the world is that obsequious or trendy charlatans tend to fare better under its benign umbrella than they would be likely to with cultivated private patrons. The reason is, as with other bureaucratic functions, that judgements are made by groups of the untrained and the unsure; made reluctantly and only because the system has killed alternative funding.

Whether grant-assisted or not, artists are increasingly treated as businessmen at a time when they are least equipped so to function. Researchers or apprentices to do hack work, or servants for domestic chores, are absurd anachronisms. Never have the integrity and professional competence of business advisers – accountants, lawyers, agents – been less favourably regarded. Never have even successful artists, through taxation, been more likely to fall off the swings and lurch off the roundabouts of their income. The cries of a contemporary composer will find echoes: 'He ripped open drawers bulging with files, cash books, and reviews. "Look at this junk! How can I work when I have to keep this up? I'm not an accountant, a press clippings service, a typist. This is what they want apparently, not music." '[1] A mediocratic composer would be happy to oblige.

[1] Frances Kelly, 'David Ahern is fed up', in *The National Times* (Sydney), 25 February–2 March 1974.

CHAPTER TWELVE

Decline and Fall
of Liberalism

*'With its basic tenets discredited and its predilections abandoned,
it is hardly surprising that liberalism has experienced a decline and
fall. . . . Whether claiming descent from, or vowing opposition to,
liberalism, its successors have one thing in common. They are all
ornaments of the mediocracy.'*

Among contemporary trends which cannot be traced from the
eighteenth century is the decline and fall of liberalism, for liberalism emerged in that century, rose in the nineteenth and peaked in
the early twentieth before its descent began. No attempt will here
be made to separate philosophical liberalism with a small 'l' and
political Liberalism with a large one. While many Liberals had
scant devotion to liberalism, the creed was influential among
other political groupings. In its heyday Conservatives supported
– or did not dare to oppose – many of its tenets, while many
trade-union leaders marched behind red flags at demonstrations
in their youth but were content to sit as Liberal parliamentarians
or ministers in later life.

As a political label Liberalism flourished in few countries
outside the United Kingdom, but so influential was Britain when
she really ruled the waves and a quarter of the earth that British
attitudes often prevailed in the absence of British institutions.
Indeed, it may be said that it was successful imitation of Britain
– in terms of trade and industry, navigation and empire-building
– rather than opposition to her, which ultimately led to her
impoverishment and eclipse. While allowing for the infinite
diversity of tribal or national histories and social customs round

the world, we may still speak of liberalism (or Liberalism) in an international context.

The two most fundamental liberal assumptions were a belief in liberty and a belief in progress, linked by a conviction that each fortified the other. If people were free to pursue their own well-being and that of associations freely entered into, overall advances would be made by society. And as society advanced, its gross national product multiplied, the share available to each individual increased – even if some got vastly more than others – and improved housing, schools and hospitals liberated minds and bodies further. Essentially, liberalism was an optimistic creed; and if there is one characteristic which entitles the 'new liberalism' of radical chic to this banner at all it is its basic optimism, whatever the evidence that might temper this today. The 'old' liberals, who often called themselves radicals, had, however, other basic beliefs that seem alien to radical chic: commitment to evolution, not revolution, and devotion to free enquiry.

Because of its association with *laissez-faire* capitalism and social Darwinism, liberalism is often accused of being immoral, or at least amoral. Yet it had a clear, if unworkable, moral foundation, best expressed in a Victorian classic on 'self-help':

> The quaint old Fuller sums up in a few words the character of the true gentleman and man of action in describing that of the great admiral, Sir Francis Drake: 'Chaste in his life, just in his dealings, true of his word; merciful to those that were under him, and hating nothing so much as idlenesse; in matters especially of moment, he was never wont to rely on other men's care, how trusty or skilful soever they might seem to be, but always contemning danger, and refusing no toyl; he was wont himself to be one (who ever was a second) at every turn, where courage, skill, or industry, was to be employed.'[1]

Thus liberalism borrowed from conservatism's concept of duty and the 'Puritan ethic' of work to invest in its own concept of freedom. Nineteenth-century permissiveness was very far from self-indulgence. According to the great liberal, John Stuart Mill,

> There are also many positive acts for the benefit of others, which he may rightfully be compelled to perform... to perform certain acts of individual beneficence, such as saving a

[1] Samuel Smiles, *Self-Help; with illustrations of Character and Conduct*, London, 1859, p. 334.

fellow-creature's life, or interposing to protect the defenceless
against ill-usage, things which whenever it is obviously a
man's duty to do, he may rightfully be made responsible to
society for not doing.[1]

Mill also suggested that it was 'almost a self-evident axiom, that
the State should require and compel the education, up to a
certain standard, of every human being who is born its citizen'.[2]

While not underwriting 'living for kicks', liberalism hoped to
maximise individual freedom in a number of areas: philosophy,
religion, industry, trade, diplomacy, social welfare. From
Thomas Paine it inherited a conviction that 'when opinions are
free, either in matters of government or religion, truth will finally
and powerfully prevail'.[3] It perpetuated, if it did not invent, a
saying attributed to Voltaire: 'I do not agree with a word you
say, but I will defend to the death your right to say it.' Its
exponents were tough-minded. They did not fear controversy for
they were able in debate, resolute in facing practical consequences of theory, and adaptable if proved wrong. Their intellectual rigour was matched only by their moral courage. They
did not adopt new views because they were trendy or refuse to
adopt them because they were nasty. They sought neither
oligarchic approval nor popular acclaim and their greatest hum-
bug was to espouse as 'popular' views that would not always
have fared well in public opinion polls. Whatever reception might
await their beliefs in manor, manse or midden, they believed in
wide dissemination through free assembly, free discussion and a
free press. Applying these principles to science and religion, they
favoured free enquiry which either led to freethought or insisted
on the rights of the individual conscience. They therefore
opposed dogmatic creeds like Roman Catholicism, preferred
Low-Church Evangelicalism to High-Church Romanism in the
Church of England, and had a close association with Nonconformism. While not always happy about public (i.e. private)
schools, they accepted the public-school, 'Muscular-Christianity'
ideal of *mens sana in corpore sano.* Many of them supported the
temperance movement and, on religious or moral or medical

1 *On Liberty*, p. 24.
2 Ibid., pp. 188–9.
3 Conclusion of *The Age of Reason* (*The Writings of Thomas Paine*), New
York and London, 1894–6, ed. Moncure Conway, Vol. IV, p. 195.

grounds, opposed the use of any drug that inhibited free rumi-
nation. Though they thought that women, children and other
'weak' sections of society should get legislative protection, they
believed in free market forces and free bargaining in the regulation of prices and adult male incomes. On the international
scene they were similarly convinced that free trade would aid
efficiency and ultimately prosperity among trading partners.
They believed that free diplomacy would often bring negotiated
settlements. In their search for peace, just as they were willing to
accept compulsory arbitration in industrial disputes, so they
came to see scope for it in international disputes. On welfare
questions their desire for reform was sometimes in conflict with
their hope for 'retrenchment'. They opposed taxes to support an
intrusive State, even if it were a Welfare State, and advocated co-
operative societies as the best means of protecting consumer,
health, assurance and welfare interests. In their view legislation
should not create special privileges for minorities, whether they
be hereditary privilegentsias or underprivileged. This is the
liberalism which was one of the forces in the rise of democracy
and flourished for a time till defeated by its other forces. Though
many liberals sought a classless society through social mobility,
in retrospect liberalism appears the creed of the intellectual
bourgeoisie, and its modern decline (whatever the fate of political
parties which claim the name) has paralleled the decline of both
the intellectual and the bourgeoisie.

This dual decline is in fact one of the chief causes of the
decline and fall of liberalism. No longer does the world seem
amenable to reason or bourgeois objectivity. Insistent cries for
'freedom' almost constitute liberophilia, but it has come adrift
from the pursuit of progress mediated by hard work, devotion to
duty and free enquiry, self-help and self-reliance. Almost all the
political and social goals of liberalism have been overtaken by
events. Free enquiry is at a discount. Those who oppose change
hold it in understandable suspicion, while those who want
change are convinced they already know what is wrong with the
world and do not want rational debate to question or hinder their
solutions. Even where free expression of opinion is permitted,
there is declining conviction in a world of admass and pressure
groups that truth will finally and powerfully prevail.

Moral courage is also at a discount. Few people would fight to
a bloody nose, let alone to the death, for the rights of opponents.
Reformers have become tender-minded, desperate for media

approval and popular acclaim as humanitarians. With the most benevolent feelings in the world they are busy glamorising criminals, defending the feckless, belittling excellence, deploring competition, blessing the bloody-minded and, as populations explode, reorganising welfare benefits to encourage professional breeders. In a world dominated by television there is so little public assembly or discussion it hardly matters whether it is free. Something similar may be said of the press, which has lost in quality and independence what it has not lost in quantity. Fiscal policy has made it difficult for constructive science to compete with destructive technology, or freethought to compete with religion. Among religious sects the collapse of authority has particularly affected those with little authority to lose, while those which support effective family planning suffer demographic decline compared with those which oppose it. Anglicanism and Nonconformism have therefore declined in relation to Roman Catholicism. In Britain the process has been accelerated by continuing Irish immigration. The disasters of American prohibition and failures of British temperance societies have given alcohol a new lease of life, while other drugs and self-indulgence boosted by the media have fostered the ideal of *mens obscura in corpore fracto*. Nationally and internationally, in industry, commerce, or diplomacy, free negotiations and arbitration are of little consequence since no one has the slightest intention of honouring any agreement which does not suit him. Through mismanagement and the failure of democratically elected committees to respond to changing economic circumstances as effectively as big business, the co-operative movement is in sad disarray. In both socialist and non-socialist countries, 'class struggle' has become a perpetual – and debilitating – fact of life.

With its basic tenets discredited and its predilections abandoned, it is hardly surprising that liberalism has experienced a decline and fall. In the resultant shake-out some unpleasant mill-owners and expendable pseudo-intellectuals may have vanished; but it is clear that there has also been a submergence of groups that were able, industrious, thoughtful, objective, creative and consistent. Whatever might be said of them, they were not mediocre. Their eclipse has undoubtedly assisted the advancement of very different people: inept, idle, thoughtless, subjective, derivative and fickle. They have replaced reformism with 'protest movements' and effective evolution with unresolved revolution. The sloppier their opinions, the more intolerant they are; the sillier, the more dogmatic. This much may be said of the 'spiritual heirs' of liberalism. But the decline and fall of any movement also advantages its natural foes: in this case, reactionaries and obscurantists. Whether claiming descent from, or vowing opposition to, liberalism, its successors have one thing in common. They are all ornaments of the mediocracy.

CHAPTER THIRTEEN

Rise of Sociology

'Sociology is fast becoming the most suspect of the sciences, the least liberal of the liberal arts and the most undisciplined of all academic disciplines. . . . Sociology becomes an expensive way of giving verisimilitude to speculation or telling the world what everyone already knows.'

The 'free enquiry' which slumped with the decline and fall of liberalism is very different from sociological studies, which are fairly booming. Born in the fertile brain of Auguste Comte, sociology had a mongrel origin which has withstood modern attempts to endow it with a pedigree. 'The science of Society,' said Comte, 'besides being more important than any other, supplies the only logical and scientific link by which all our varied observations of phenomena can be brought into one consistent whole.'[1] In his writings sociology became confounded with 'Positivism', which 'consists essentially of a Philosophy and a Polity', believes in 'systematically separating political from moral government' and 'implies a union of the social aspirations of the Middle Ages with the wise political instincts of the Convention'.[2] Though not believing in God, Comte 'long ago repudiated all philosophical and historical connection between Positivism and what is called Atheism', and his historical observ-

[1] Auguste Comte, *A General View of Positivism; or Summary Exposition of the System of Thought and Life, adapted to the Great Western Republic, formed of the five advanced nations, the French, Italian, Spanish, British, and German, which, since the time of Charlemagne, have always constituted a political whole* (1851 ed.) tr. J. H. Bridges, London, 1880, p. 1.
[2] Ibid., pp. 1 and 67.

ations were so acute that he was able to describe the Vatican's long record of corruption and power politics as 'the great effort of Catholicism, to bring Western Europe to a social system of peaceful activity and intellectual culture, in which Thought and Action should be subordinated to universal art'.[1] Since there is little purpose in liturgy without thaumaturgy, Positivism failed like other 'Religions of Humanity' but sociology has gone on from strength to strength.

While it is important to study the mechanics of society before trying to assess its real needs or introduce new ideas, sociology is fast becoming the most suspect of the sciences, the least liberal of the liberal arts and the most undisciplined of all academic disciplines. Not only is it, like all trendy subjects, more than usually vulnerable to academic politicking, it has shown great capacity to get caught up in politics itself. Like economics, it has not been content to fracture into the crazed surface of conflicting theories which many sciences present to the world, but has split into a 'right wing' and a 'left wing'. The 'right' seeks to preserve the *status quo* by representing the state of society as a resultant of opposing forces; the 'left' seeks radical change by claiming that existing society is not satisfying ascertainable human needs and wants. On one side there is a belief that sociology is descriptive, independently cataloguing moral aspirations and political realities; on the other, that sociology is prescriptive, citing moral aspirations to challenge political realities. Since the subject appeals to the youthful idealism of undergraduates who know little about it but feel the older professions are hidebound and 'irrelevant' to human needs, the left flourishes in the junior common rooms and lower teaching ranks at universities, whose 'student protest' and riots traditionally incubate in schools of sociology. There are also practical reasons for this, since the trendiness of the subject has made sociology the most over-crowded and understaffed of university faculties. It has the further distinction of being a prime breeding-ground for cynicism and disillusion, since its graduates are more likely to become market researchers for multinational detergent corporations than propagandists for freedom fighters.

In any mediocracy those loudest in proclaiming the 'irrel-evance' of others are most likely to be irrelevant themselves. Sociologists are fond of describing as scientific 'tools' what

[1] Ibid., pp. 33 and 67.

scarcely rate as playthings, as 'value-free' approaches what would better be called valueless, and as 'true' samples what are false pictures. Quite apart from political axes which seem in constant need of grinding, social prejudices of every kind glint among the ranks of professional sociologists. All of them may look forward to fulfilment, since sociological 'findings' – like adultery – prosper where motive and opportunity are maximised. In few other disciplines are researchers more anxious to prove what they already believe, and few others offer such convenient means of doing so. Controlled experiments in a 'live' situation effectively kill it; questionnaires turn scientific questions into leading questions capable of any and every inaccurate answer; trend-curves are the perfect way of imprisoning the future in a crystal of the past. With the possible exception of economics, no subject is more dependent on psychology and more unconscious of this dependence. It discovers people's wants while believing it has discovered their needs and it discovers their interpretation of society's expectations while believing it has discovered their expectations of society. By impeccable statistical means, calculated to the third decimal place, it conceives social errors that would never be fathered by a novelist or poet unable to add up his grocery bill.

There are of course occasions when sociologists accurately conduct and interpret surveys. Here at least, it will be said, valuable information is provided. Sometimes, yes. But is it always? More perhaps than other facts, a sociological 'fact' is meaningless in isolation. One needs to know its antecedents and its concomitants. Yet in studying society 'all our varied observations of phenomena' do not necessarily survey all phenomena, while our 'observations' of them, which are eminently subjective, are rarely 'consistent'. When it is not politicising, sociology often claims 'value-free' approaches to things which are not value-free; and, by sponsoring equal veneration of all beliefs, opinions and wants, has aided the decline and fall of the intellectual. At other times, by exhaustive investigation sociology establishes what few would dispute: that tall people are more likely to excel at basketball than short people, that poor people fear inflation more than rich people, that young people travel more than old people. In other words, sociology becomes an expensive way of giving verisimilitude to speculation or telling the world what everyone already knows.

In parapsychology one may find sciences that are more bogus.

More money is profitlessly spent on the space programme. Mediocrities can readily find easier options. Sociology warrants special attention in tracing the rise of the mediocracy for other reasons. It is the fastest growing of all university disciplines. From the universities it has spread to the schools.

> One of the worst services educationalists have performed in recent years is lumping the subjects of history, geography and economics in primary and early secondary schools into that cloying mess called 'social studies'. Social studies led naturally to a laziness of thought and a type of glibness of approach best seen in that scourge of parents and pamphlet producers, the project.[1]

It has produced a caricature of the scientific method, made mathematical formulae a substitute for thought, and filled learned journals with tedious trivia. Privacy is invaded and re-invaded in endless investigations, where the existence of God gains the same sort of status as preference in paper handkerchiefs. Yes, says the beleaguered slum-dweller, he has heard of slums, he lives in a slum, he doesn't like it and for Christ's sake what's going to be done about it? That, says the sociologist, left-wing or right-wing, is not a question for sociologists. Positivism claimed to have separated political from moral government. Logical positivism suggested moral government was meaningless nonsense. Sociology has made meaningless nonsense out of political government, smothering it with ill-digested, ill-dissected and ill-directed facts and fictions, strangling it with unrewarding jargon or drowning it in pious sentiment. Morality has been confused with aesthetics and both with social engineering, which cannot create harmony in sociology faculties but advertises it for the world. At one time sociologists seem too busy asking questions to look for answers, at another too busy dispensing answers to ask questions. The intellectual and practical solutions it has provided for the real problems of the world mark sociology out as the ideological wing of the mediocracy. They are growing together impressively.

[1] Editorial in *The Australian Financial Review*, 5 March 1974.

CHAPTER FOURTEEN

'The Medium is the Message'

'Belief that "the medium is the message" ... has made every conceptual distinction of no greater consequence than the veneer on a television set. ... Mediocrities ... now face the future confident that their torch of imperishable hackwork can be preserved and passed on to future generations.'

In a world of 'images' things are influential both for what they are and for what they are assumed to be. It was particularly to be expected that the media should elicit a cult of the media which would go a long way towards obscuring what they were in fact doing. This cult originated with a Canadian professor, who seemed at first to have a very different message: 'Since so many minds are engaged in bringing about this condition of public helplessness, and since these programmes of commercial education are so much more expensive and influential than the relatively puny offerings sponsored by schools and colleges, it seemed fitting to devise a method for reversing the process.'[1] Such ambitions might well stir to arms the highbrow social studies master whose proudest boast was that he did not himself own a television set and whose daily fulminations against admass convinced his pupils that it must be more attractive than they had hitherto thought. 'A film expert', the message continued, 'speaking of the value of the movie medium for selling North to South America, noted that: "the propaganda value of this simultaneous audio-visual impression is very high, for it standardises thought by supplying the spectator with a ready-made visual

[1] Marshall McLuhan, *The Mechanical Bride. Folklore of Industrial Man*, Toronto, 1951, Preface.

image before he has time to conjure up an interpretation of his own." ' Expanded in further books, however, the message took on very different, and not altogether consistent, overtones.

According to the new cult – a worthy neophilia – social dislocation and anomie came about not through technology as such but certain types of technology, ancient and relatively modern. The first was writing. 'Until writing was invented, man lived in acoustic space: boundless, directionless, horizonless.'[1] Things were not so bad when writing consisted of hieroglyphs or ideograms on stone, before the invention of paper and the alphabet. 'The phonetic alphabet reduced the use of all the senses at once, which is oral speech, to a merely visual code.'[2] During the Middle Ages the line of 'linear' communication was happily broken, but the Renaissance compounded the impact of the alphabet by the invention (in the West) of printing. 'The alphabet and print technology fostered and encouraged a fragmenting process, a process of specialism and of detachment.'[3] And with the invention of photography, the gramophone, film and radio, even electric light and the waltz, this process continued. But latterday help was at hand. Fortifying the good work of the telephone, television and the electronic revolution returned man to his 'primitive' origins. 'Automation creates roles for people, which is to say depth of involvement in their work and human association that our preceding mechanical technology had destroyed.'[4] Briefly, 'Electric technology fosters and encourages unification and involvement.'[5]

The key to 'understanding media' is recognition of whether or not they are hot or cool. 'A hot medium is one that extends one single sense in "high definition". High definition is the state of being well filled with data.... Hot media are, therefore, low in participation, and cool media are high in participation or completion by the audience.'[6] Among hot media are listed the phonetic alphabet, paper, lecture, waltz, photography, gramophone, film and radio: among cool, hieroglyphs or ideogrammic writing, stone, seminar, jazz, cartoon, telephone, speech and tele-

---

[1] McLuhan, *The Medium is the Massage*, p. 48.
[2] McLuhan, *The Gutenberg Galaxy: the making of typographical man*, Toronto, 1962, p. 45.
[3] *The Medium is the Massage*, p. 8.
[4] McLuhan, *Understanding Media: The Extensions of Man*, London, 1964, p. 7.
[5] *The Medium is the Massage*, p. 8.
[6] *Understanding Media*, pp. 22–3.

vision. Why radio is divorced from 'acoustic space', television from a 'visual code', and film and television from each other when a substantial part of television output consists of old movies, are not entirely clear. Indeed, one might think there would be more 'involvement' and 'participation' seeing a film among a heterogeneous crowd at a cinema than watching it at home with the family or alone. But there are other anomalies in this analysis which can only comfort the mediocracy.

If every cult has a slogan, that of the modern media is 'The Medium is the Message'. It was originally the title of the first chapter of *Understanding Media: The Extensions of Man* and has flourished ever since, though its author may have had some misgivings which prompted him to call a later book *The Medium is the Massage*. Behind the slogan is a concept which has some validity:

> This is merely to say that the personal and social consequences of any medium – that is, of any extension of ourselves – result from the new scale that is introduced into our affairs by each extension of ourselves, or by any new technology. . . . In terms of the way in which the machine altered our relations to one another and to ourselves, it mattered not in the least whether it turned out cornflakes or Cadillacs.[1]

Passing from industrial processes to the media of communications, most people will agree that 'it is impossible to understand social and cultural changes without a knowledge of the workings of media': but it is one thing to accept that, another to believe that 'societies have always been shaped more by the nature of the media by which men communicate than by the content of the communication',[2] and yet another to agree that the medium is the message. After the invention of writing it was possible to draw up enduring contracts and inventories, invoices and bills of lading, to codify laws and establish 'religions of the book'. It is hard to envisage cities, empires and large-scale trading without it. Yet the Incas developed their civilisation on a foundation of illiteracy, and there appears to be a greater difference in the laws, customs, religious and life-styles of literate communities than among 'primitive' peoples round the world.

Belief that 'the medium is the message' has not only promoted

1 *Understanding Media*, pp. 7 and 8.
2 *The Medium is the Massage*, p. 8.

the decline and fall of the intellectual, it has made every conceptual distinction of no greater consequence than the veneer on
a television set. It has spread the myth that the more people one
communicates with the more effective is the 'communication'. It
has created a class of professional 'communicators' who are not
trained writers or speakers or apprentices to any particular craft,
who have no special wisdom or experience or settled opinions,
but who are taken seriously because they are there and are
featured today for no better reason than that they were featured
yesterday. They have made every serious subject – especially
politics – an extension of showbiz and every public image more
important than public policy. They are both the masters and the
slaves of 'public opinion', which can be readily manipulated by
market researchers and analysts, which when it is truly
spontaneous often represents the most unconsidered or ill-
considered views and the strongest prejudices, but which may be
nothing more than jet-set chatter or journalistic gossip. At
irregular intervals a consensus of media mediocrats decides that
a particular communicator is 'over-exposed' and he plunges
from view. Happily there are abundant replacements at hand. As
in the space programme, which fits its men to its machines and
not its machines to its men, these reserves all lie within the
acceptable range of physical, mental and moral characteristics. A
few years ago 'many people would be disposed to say that it was
not the machine, but what one did with the machine, that was its
meaning or message'.[1] Today they would be disposed to say that
in every field production is the only index of life and rising
production the only index of progress.

If the cult of the media were accompanied by no social
theories, the worst it could do would be to sow a crop of
mediocre dragon's teeth that an irate populace might at any time
choose to root up. With a wise foresight, however, the cult has
brought along myths of 'involvement' and 'participation'.
Paradigm is the 'global medieval village' supposedly created by
television. Beneath the shadow of baron and bishop, squire and
parson, the Middle Ages probably offered little decision-making
to the average villager. It is certain that the operation of modern
television offers none at all. Sporadic attempts to introduce
'public access' programmes have not got beyond well-known
pressure groups sustained by a few highly articulate people, and

[1] *Understanding Media*, p. 7.

have tended to run into every sort of political and legal problem. In its ordinary operations television reaches millions with the work of a tiny handful of 'creative' people filtered by a tinier handful of programme planners. Far from rebuilding a medieval village, it has tended to destroy the 'villages' of public meetings and debating forums and erode those of the theatre and the cinema. Together with curbless crime it nightly confines people singly and in nuclear family groups in segregated living rooms, where not only are there no opportunities for questions or discussion but, for the most part, no televisual equivalent of the newspaper letter to the editor. Because of the concept of 'the medium is the message' and the theoretical capacity of the television camera to go everywhere and transmit simultaneously, it is readily assumed that it has gone everywhere and transmitted simultaneously. In fact it goes only where it chances to be, where it is invited or where it chooses to go; while technical reasons, if no other, ensure that many programmes are telerecorded and edited some time before they appear. Because of the very limited time slot for news and current affairs, more editing, tendentious or otherwise, occurs in this medium than in any other, and it shares with the cinema an ability to cheat with the most open face in the world. Naturally it goes to great pains to establish an aura of objectivity and immediacy, and if it is rarely able to give an instant broadcast of an important event where this is desirable, it is never lacking in an instant opinion where this is not desirable. Not surprisingly, this myth of physical involvement culminates in a myth of moral involvement.

> Western man acquired from the technology of literacy the power to act without reacting.... We acquired the art of carrying out the most dangerous social operations with complete detachment. . . . It is no longer possible to adopt the aloof and dissociated role of the literate Westerner.... The aspiration of our time for wholeness, empathy and depth of awareness is a natural adjunct of electric technology.[1]

An aspiration, yes. The reason why it is so strong is that the achievement is so remote. Electric press-button warfare has made combatants less involved, both physically and emotionally, in the consequences of their actions. The same may be said of opinionating before electric cameras and microphones.

[1] Ibid., pp. 4 and 5.

What is true of television is true of other media. In local arts centres and 'community' halls the most jejune painting, sculpture, music, poetry and 'mixed media' events see the daunting light of day in the name of 'participation'. The highest aim of art is, it is said, to conceal art; and contemporary exponents conceal it very well indeed. But is there an infinity of hanging space, stage space, display space or hours to the day in these outlets of supposed participation? Or, rather, are they not dominated by sundry cliques, coteries and local 'personalities' who follow the bouncing requirements of admass rather than the languishing requirements of their crafts? Supported by the public purse, mediocrities no longer depend on their own resources or those of friends and relations, which were exhaustible. They now face the future confident that their torch of imperishable hackwork can be preserved and passed on to future generations.

Universal mediocrity has become a universal mediocracy.

Part Two

Practical

CHAPTER FIFTEEN

Redundant Religion

'*Saints and martyrs, heretics and apostates have been rescued from burning faggots by the extinction of burning beliefs. . . . The eucharist has as much magic and majesty as Saturday night at the local* discothèque. . . . *The Hierarchy can claim to be little but the richest, greediest, surliest and stupidest mediocracy in the world.*'

In an unashamedly 'hot' medium it is appropriate to pass from theory to practice in 'linear' progression. At the level of personal awareness, however, the rise of the mediocracy first impinges practically. For, in the world of the mind, the theory of evolution, expanding education and social services, discoveries in genetics, eugenics and psychology, industrial arbitration and international agencies might all lead one to a facile optimism, or a pessimism evoked by the deeds of a scheming minority but tempered by contemplation of the decency and good sense of 'ordinary' people. No one wants to be like

> . . . the idiot who praises, with enthusiastic tone,
> All centuries but this, and every country but his own.[1]

Much less, in an age of juvenilophilia, does one want to be thought an ageing malcontent. Yet declining standards, social disruption and militant ugliness force themselves on our attention till they can no longer be ignored. Unless one believes in black magic or the 'last days' beloved of overheated hot-gospellers, one looks for antecedents and influences behind

[1] W. S. Gilbert, *The Mikado; or The Town of Titipu*, London, 1885, Act I.

modern trends. Then the social causes of our present situation become apparent. Though masked, for a time, by contrary factors, they turn out to have been active for a considerable period. Their study is an interesting one; but we return to practical issues as more obtrusive and, for some – if only a dwindling minority – more vexatious.

Religion is a suitable starting-point, not because it is central in the lives of many people today but because it was once central in their lives and in society, has drifted to a psychological extremity, yet retains prominence in the legal system, privilege in the fiscal system and power in the educational system. Its redundance is clearly not a social one but an intellectual one, not a political one in a pressure-group sense but a political one in an architectonic sense. There is, briefly, no need to invoke religion to explain first and last causes or uphold law, order and morality.

Once the clergy functioned as more than priests. However imperfectly or insufficiently, they were society's fortune-tellers and whoremasters, clerks and lawyers, social workers and administrators, educators and doctors. If their ministrations had little impact on society they had a big impact on themselves. In things both spiritual and temporal priests had status befitting their supposed powers. The priesthood was regarded as a learned profession, its studies the 'queen of the sciences'. At times illegitimate sons gained unearnt elevation, and nephews were a perpetual hazard, but celibacy usually ensured constant replenishment (turban renewal) with fresh blood. When the Church had a monopoly on education, bright young men had little alternative but to accept her holy embrace. Mediocrities might join them but no hereditary mediocracy was able to flourish and clerics of great brilliance were not uncommon into the nineteenth century.

It is a very different situation today. Now 'the intellectual and pastoral abilities of the bishops reflect pretty fairly the age of mediocrity in which we live'.[1] If the bishop is a good business manager everyone in the diocese is more than content. And if the parish priest can manage on his stipend, not seek too many faculties from church courts and not live in open and notorious sin with the local headmistress, his parishioners think they have a treasure. The reason is that the second-oldest profession is not what it used to be. Its jargon grows increasingly arcane and increasingly incredible, its fancy-dress looks weirder the more

[1] Michael De-la-Noy, *A Day in the Life of God*, London, 1971, p. 87.

people forget its symbolism, its social status is inferior to that of the more 'practical' professions and – save at the top – its earning potential has declined accordingly. Statutory bodies have taken over its bureaucratic functions and the universities its academic functions. Even its priestly functions are suffering stiff competition from do-it-yourself alternatives. Despite the decline and fall of the intellectual, it is possible for organisations to suffer an intellectual crisis. At bottom, this is what has overtaken the Church.

Religious debate is increasingly denatured. Save in the broadest terms, few clerics would now care to challenge atheists to disputation on theology and biblical scholarship (and few atheists would care to accept the challenge). Debate has been replaced by 'dialogue', where protagonists take few beliefs into, and incomprehension out of, bland and lengthy discussions. So attenuated has genuine belief become that we now have, for example, Zen Catholicism, Catholic Marxism and Catholic Humanism. Reconciling the irreconcilable in this area has been hailed as a manifestation of divine grace when it should have been dismissed as a compromise of the shallowly committed. Saints and martyrs, heretics and apostates have been rescued from burning faggots by the extinction of burning beliefs. Philosophical religion and irreligion are so dead that no one could frame a convincing charge or mount a coherent defence at any inquisition. Intolerance has been replaced by insouciance. The rise of democracy has reduced overt persecution less by undermining bigotry than by undermining conviction.

Though its Pontiff continues to pontificate on 'faith and morals' – and whatever politics he feels disposed to support or denounce – Roman Catholicism is becoming as irrelevant in most Catholic countries as Protestantism is in Protestant countries. The faithful will follow their priests when it means securing financial and other privileges at the expense of tax-paying majorities or devotional minorities, not when it interferes with their own sexual or social convenience. While it has little to say to the mind, the sacrifice of the mass (unless it is a 'rock' mass) has less to say to the heart. With catarrhal celebrants facing the congregation, accelerated responses taking as little time as possible out of the fun-loving observance of the Lord's Day, and Gregorian chants designed for the flowing measures of Latin now twisted and tortured into the vernacular, the eucharist has as much magic and majesty as Saturday night at the local *discothèque*. Few laymen confess more often than strict formalism demands and, if they want counselling, are far more likely to go to a lawyer or psychiatrist, marriage guidance counsellor or social worker, than to their parish priest. With no obligation on its professionals to be scholars or actors, or on its amateurs to be faithful or abstemious, Catholicism is becoming as much of a charade as its old enemy, Freemasonry. Mediocre in both its message and its ministry, stripped of the most charismatic and lucrative of its saints (who are now accused of doubtful historicity), berated for its sexual hangups, exposed in its business dealings, and finding even the bleeding heart of Jesus and the immaculate heart of Mary less productive in tears and contributions, the Hierarchy can claim to be little but the richest, greediest, surliest and stupidest mediocracy in the world.

Within the ranks of Christianity outside the One, Holy, Catholic and Apostolic Church of Rome, only 'Greek' Orthodoxy is more venerably dated and sonorously titled. But so divided and eroded by political disruption within its traditional sphere of influence has it become, that its mediocrity scarcely ranks as a mediocracy. Its largest offshoot, Russian Orthodoxy, has both the cross and the crown of absorption into the Communist Party apparatus, so that while it is hardly a force in its own right it preserves for itself a corner in a mediocracy of formidable dimensions. Among world religions Protestantism is particularly pathetic. Its God has died, its Jesus is reduced to the status of an 'angry young man' – if not of a sacred mushroom – its salesmen are eloquent only on the subject of their stipends and its bible is continually retranslated into language of the thinnest banality. Seeds of intellectual decay and organisational disarray were present in the Reformation, and brought an early harvest of religious 'enthusiasm' and fanaticism to Europe. The twentieth century has provided a particularly favourable climate for this growth, which has spread throughout the world. Reason has yielded to revelation, fact to faith, works to worship of increasing incoherence, verbal testimony to glossolalia. Where Christianity is deemed not to be 'religionless' its religion is described as 'experiential'. Anarchic intuition and mysticism have ceased to be an 'optional extra' and become the chief commodity. 'Jesus freaks' is no longer a term of abuse but a chosen denomination. Trendy Protestantism is an extension of hippie subculture, whose neophilia is as likely to produce a new sectarian position as a new sexual position.

Not surprisingly, searching spirits in the West have, since nineteenth-century comparative studies brought them to notice, turned to other religions. At neither its ideological nor its organisational level has Judaism proved particularly inviting (and it is only recently that converts have, in modern circumstances, been accepted at all) though the radical chic have made Zionism and vacations on *kibbutzim* eminently fashionable. Idiosyncratic Islam has gained a great hold on westernised Negroes and Sufism a certain following among whites who have tried everything else. But the occult and the East have been chief beneficiaries of the decline of Christianity, and rich are the offerings of antique and eastern bazaars.

Evolutionary meritocrats of the nineteenth century believed, in their optimism, that there was an evolution of ideas whereby new knowledge bore new insights and killed old ones. They forgot that biological evolution is not unidirectional and that modern variations of the most primitive forms of life have continued to live side.by side with multicellular extravaganzas. At all events the twentieth century has demonstrated that intellectual mediocracy is eternal. Monotheism has not supplanted polytheism; polytheism, animism; religion, magic. Nothing is too old to be discredited, just as nothing is too new to gain credit. And if the superstition had been thought to be extinct until recently revived, neophilia fortifies primitivophilia. Freemasonry and Rosicrucianism have been joined by demonology, witchcraft, black and white magic, Druidism and Satanism in preserving our pre-Christian heritage. In the most respectable suburbs one may find spiritualistic seances, faith-healing clinics and witches' covens, together with astrologers, clairvoyants, tea-cup readers and tarot-card interpreters. Space programmes are said to include telepathy for extraterrestrial communication, and unidentified flying objects play the same role today as comets did in the Middle Ages. Only the creature's rarity and conservationist pressure prevent divination by studying the flight or the entrails of an eagle. A potentially sympathetic observer of the occult industry has concluded:

Another kind of sign-seekers are the people fascinated with psychic powers, believing that all genuine mystics must also be magicians who can remember their past lives, foretell the future, read other people's thoughts, heal diseases, and travel about in their astral bodies. Though I am open to the possibility of such powers I have never seen them exercised (excepting a man who walked on fire and the phenomenon of hypnosis), and it has always struck me that most of the magical feats reported are trivial. The wizards make high scores on ESP cards, read questions in sealed envelopes, cause vases to fall off shelves, project pictures on films by mental concentration, or materialise flowers, jewels, and other baubles out of the air. No one so materialises tons of rice for starving Indians, and of all the prominent astrologers only one or two predicted the actual outbreak of World War II.[1]

The Orient is the strongest rival of the occult. On its exotic shores one may derive inspiration from the 'collection of amiable platitudes' that constitute Bahai and the 'adolescent rituals' of Zen Buddhism.[2] Above all, one may stroll happily from *guru* to *guru* absorbing ' "Krishna-consciousness" and Transcendental Meditation and all this nonsense that is going on'.[3] That is, if one can track them down and afford space at their feet. For these spiritual beacons jet round the world lauding the virtues of quietude, put up at five-star hotels to extol the simple life, and speak and write copiously of the inadequacy of language. Everywhere they are accompanied by disciples who explain their cat-naps as trances and their physiological processes as *maya*. Everything we value – especially our money – is illusory, and they are happy to take our illusions from us. Truly, 'all *gurus* are phoney, you can take that for granted right from the beginning, whether they are Tibetan Lamas or Catholics, or Hindus'.[4] Outside their native habitat they are not yet numerous enough to form a mediocracy, but they have become the intimates of mediocrats and established cults of verbiage, unreason, social apathy and parasitism which have greatly aided the rise of the mediocracy.

[1] Alan Watts, *In My Own Way*, pp. 150–1.
[2] Ibid., pp. 252 and 120.
[3] Krishnamurti, *The Awakening of Intelligence*, p. 22.
[4] Ibid., p. 192.

CHAPTER SIXTEEN

Pusillanimous Politics

'The "new revolutionaries" are more active on the media of other countries than on the battlefields of their own. . . . Most nations are unhappy enough under their own mediocracies without seeking subservience to a lowest common multiple of international mediocracies.'

With the collapse of systems and authority, the decline and fall of liberalism and the rise of bureaucracy, the 'democratic process' is in difficulties. In the parliamentary democracies power is increasingly vested outside Parliament: in the Civil Service, boardrooms of multinational corporations, offices of the big trades unions. Some of these institutions hold elections, but successful candidates at best represent sectional rather than community interests, while it is questionable to what extent directors are really accountable to shareholders or trade union officers to their rank and file. Within the parliamentary orbit it is the Executive – however elected or theoretically accountable to other politicians – rather than the Legislature which has effective power. In everyday matters,

> When in that House MPs divide,
> If they've a brain and cerebellum, too,
> They've got to leave that brain outside,
> And vote just as their leaders tell 'em to.[1]

If parliamentary pressures have turned members into

[1] W. S. Gilbert, *Iolanthe; or The Peer and the Peri*, London, 1882, Act II

mediocrities, their leaders have become mediocrats. Theirs is a particular talent to be prototype 'common men', television creations or ideological weather-vanes. Above all, they must come to terms with the local constituency apparatus and the national party machine, especially if they have limited personal means. To have intellectual aspirations would condemn them as arrogant; to have moral courage, contemptuous of public opinion; to have political principles, inflexible. Instead they need dry palms for hand-shaking, fresh breath for baby-kissing and folksy voices for television-pleading. With good makeup girls, speech-writers and publicity men, they do not need to trouble about platforms or policies. A criminal record is a disadvantage; but moral scruples are more disadvantageous. 'It is not those with the best natures but those with the worst who are most favourably equipped to win', says one insider. 'A willingness unfairly to strike down a rival, to betray one's principles, to pander to the majority, to conceal the truth and actually to tell lies whenever expediency suggests, are often essential weapons for victory in the power struggle for the supreme office.... It is getting the job of Prime Minister which is difficult, not doing it.'[1]

Despite the political patronage – which may extend to diplomatic, judicial or ecclesiastical appointments that endure when the patron has fallen from power – that resides in the Executive, elections must be faced. Usually they rear up before long-term policies (should such exist) in foreign affairs or economics have a chance to mature. As the country must be made to seem diplomatically and economically strong, overseas concessions and internal austerity must be abandoned. At all costs the economy must be inflated; and all costs are generally involved. If elections are not at fixed times the government is perennially sensitive to the risk of being 'brought down' and every vote tends to be a vote of 'confidence'. It is not only matters of national moment that have members scuttling out of toilets or carried in on sick beds to satisfy party whips. Much less are they matters where the member has a clear brief from his constituents.

A number of consequences flow from these conditions of public life. It has come to attract those with infinite patience for trivia, intrigue and tricks, those who see politics as an extension of show business or other business, those who see the status of 'lobby fodder' as a necessary prelude to that of national leader.

1 Woodrow Wyatt, *Turn Again, Westminster*, London, 1973, pp. 185, 193.

Clearly, only a certain type of person will accept such conditions of 'service'. The meritocrats are fleeing, the mediocrats are moving in. Yet such is the cussedness of human nature that 'common men' object to being governed by men who are equally common but much better paid. They object to a two-party system where each party, in cultivating the middle ground, has become indistinguishable from its rival and represents nothing but an alternative juggernaut, and to systems of proportional representation where innumerable minority parties enter and leave permanently impermanent coalitions.

They are, in short, increasingly contemptuous of politics and politicians. It is not surprising, therefore, that throughout the world there are barracks always listening for the call of irate or ambitious colonels to overthrow 'corrupt and inefficient' parliamentary democracy, and public reaction inside most military dictatorships is minimal. 'Freedom' is not the only, and is probably not the chief, human aspiration.

So far the older, more liberal 'liberal democracies' have eluded the rule of the colonels. Here popular discontent, especially among the younger generation, takes the form of protest movements, 'underground' newspapers, the 'alternative society' and the 'counter-culture'. Unlike the revolutionaries of old, these warriors for anti-politics will do anything for their ideas except codify them and anything for their beliefs except suffer for them. Comfortably supported by the welfare state or middle-class parents, whom they constantly denounce, they sometimes qualify as 'utopian socialists' by supporting communes of traditional longevity (about eighteen months) and sometimes escape political opposition by supporting nothing at all. In so far as it is possible to extract from hazy harangues a non-party platform for the alternative society, supporters are urged to fuck, fix, finish work and freak out. Happily, those impatient with elected politicians and non-elected multinational corporations alike may make empiric studies of the enterprises of the counter-culture and satisfy themselves whether these protesters, who offer to rule the world on our behalf, are able to run a hamburger joint on their own.

In military dictatorships and 'banana republics' protest must be made of something sterner but is seldom more coherent. 'Freedom fighters' are rarely without legitimate national grievances yet often come from a social class whose privileges are assured. But it is one thing to have idealistic motives and another

E

to have compassionate, courageous and effective techniques. The 'new revolutionaries' are more active on the media of other countries than on the battlefields of their own. That could be justified if they concentrated on reasoned arguments and empathetic appeals. Instead, their arguments are likely to become threats and their appeals to other nations suggest blackmail rather than blandishment. Only a Marxist-Leninist who had read neither Marx nor Lenin, or an unattached Leftist who had read nothing at all, could see virtue in indiscriminate car-bombs and letter-bombs, kidnapping and ransoming, hijacking and sky-jacking; for not only are their victims civilians with no individual involvement in the political situation which disturbs the freedom fighters, they have, for the most part, no collective responsibility for what happens in another country and however panicked by fear could bring little or no pressure on any government in a position to remove the basic grievance. If revolutionaries are not recognisable neurotics or psychotics, if they are too ill-organised to be described as a mediocracy, through promotion by media mediocrats round the globe they have cultivated throughout society the cult of the *acte gratuit* – an apotheosis of mindless violence, sanctimonious self-indulgence and inarticulate anarchy.

Just as the rise of technology has put into the hands of every individual fanatic lethal control over hundreds, so it has the potential to put millions to ransom by tiny nation-states or breakaway states, political factions or even crime syndicates. At the same time it has ignited a population explosion that fore-thought and self-control are too weak to contain. It should have given personal insight or at least the means of outside control, just as the rise of sociology should have promoted national in-sight and the creation of international control – a happy coalition of the carrot and the stick. Indeed, it has provided the necessary knowledge and techniques. Unfortunately it has been unable to generate the political will.

The meritocrats of the nineteenth century had an orderly blue-print for achieving human progress. They linked it to education, hard work, a sense of duty, productivity and orderly reform. Redistribution of goods would not, they said, abolish poverty if productivity fell while populations rose. 'Emancipation' would achieve no worthwhile advance individually or nationally if minds were not free and institutions were not ready for it. In the twentieth century the rise of democracy accelerated beyond, and differently from, their expectations and beyond the capacity of the world's resources and national and international institutions to satisfy the expectations of a runaway population. The franchise has spread faster than political maturity, urbanisation faster than housing expansion or agricultural development, and membership of the United Nations faster than its peace-keeping potential. Resolutions of the General Assembly and decisions of the International Court of Justice can be defied with impunity. In the absence of effective sanctions international debate may foment more dissension than it resolves. 'Moral pressure' is increasingly feeble as it becomes doubtful who has a moral *locus standi*.

Dissatisfaction with the incompetence and greed, intolerance and bellicosity of the imperialist powers of the First World has in this century turned men of good will to the socialist brotherhood of the Second World, the honest simplicity of the Third World, and the peace-loving purity of the non-aligned powers. There they hoped to find answers to the intractable problems of mankind, just as earlier centuries looked to the New World to right the injustices of the Old. It was a beautiful dream but, like most beautiful dreams in politics, never realised.

The socialist dream was based on a number of images: that the proletariat constitutes a majority; that the majority is always right; that the interests of the proletariat are the same throughout the world; that international socialism will thus bring international peace. As these theories had never been tested before the twentieth century they could not be refuted empirically. Parliamentary democracy was under a cloud.

> Lack of housing, the persistence of slums, squalid cities and desecrated countryside, glaring poverty, unemployment regarded as inevitable for a percentage of those who are capable of work, recurrent crises in the economy affecting the wage packet and the shopping basket, constant alarms and excursions in foreign affairs – all are problems the electorate are periodically assured will be solved within five years in return for their votes. All remain as bad or worse when the Government's term of office ends. Governments change but the problems remain.[1]

If manipulated democracy could be replaced by people's democracy, overlordship of the bourgeoisie by dictatorship of the proletariat, class struggle by class liquidation, five-year junketings

[1] Emanuel Shinwell, *I've Lived Through It All*, London, 1973, p. 250.

by five-year plans, and international rivalry by international co-operation, all would be well. With the establishment of people's democracies in the twentieth century empirical assessment became possible, but so attractive was the theory, biased the observers and poor the sources of information it was some time before the truth was faced. This was, briefly, that the proletariat was no more reliable a source of efficiency and integrity than any other class; that throughout the world it was as divided by national interests as the nations themselves; that a one-party state was as corrupt as, and more bureaucratic than, a two-party state; that the greater the insistence on ideological purity the greater the persecution of creative dissidents. One carefully moderate 'angry young man' of the socialist world was forced to conclude:

> Ultimately, I turned out to have been right, but already in those two cases I had personal experience of how greatly the bureacracy is irritated by the most sincere attempts to come to the defence of someone.... The truth is replaced by suppression, and suppression actually is a lie.... Our duty is to defend those who perished in Stalinist camps because they themselves can no longer speak. Our duty is to defend the living, to criticise and to help identify the right course if they make mistakes. But administrative methods and crude pressure are not means of conviction. They can only be counter-productive.[1]

He had seen the development of a monstrous mediocracy consisting – though he did not say – of men whose only claim to advancement was an impeccable working-class origin, actual or invented, who could follow the tortuosities of any party line without falling off, who judged everything in terms of political correctness and not practical efficiency, who had travelled little and had a peasant's suspicion of the outside world. In another part of the Second World society has become so politicised, so intoxicated by the 'thoughts' of its leader, so hostile to external influences and bourgeois objectivity, so determined to denature its intellectuals, that at times only the army can persuade the 'revolutionary masses' to go about their ordinary duties. The result is that these countries have to turn to capitalist 'running dogs' for basic foodstuffs and factory technology, while their able

[1] Yevgeny Yevtushenko, 'A letter to Soviet radio and television audiences', 16 February 1974.

and sensitive citizens try to escape abroad or turn in their despair to ancient philosophers or redundant religion.

Disappointed in the Second World, men of good will then lavished their hopes, or their prayers, on the Third World. Parts of this amorphous territory were recognised as intrinsically poor, but large parts of it were known or suspected to be rich in natural resources. Yet its natives remained poor, ill-nourished and ill-educated. Clearly the only explanation could be colonial exploitation. When those who had ravished their resources and their women, exchanging their land for the Bible and trinkets, magnifying their rivalries to 'divide and rule', were toppled from their imperial throne, prosperity would reign. Now they have toppled, and prosperity is as far away as ever. Of course, say apologists. Just as the Second World is held to have betrayed 'true socialism' in favour of state capitalism, so the Third World has shaken off colonialism to be ensnared by neo-colonialism operated through multinational corporations. While this is a factor of some importance, there are others no less important though rarely remarked on. In retrospect, imperialism can be seen to have introduced – along with its well-known abuses, political, economic and religious – technology and public works, however rudimentary, a Civil Service with basic standards of justice and impartiality, a legal system making some effort to protect the weak from the strong at a local level, a disinterested army alert to suppress local factionalism. At the very least, each imperial power provided an external scapegoat, a focus of universal hatred that factitiously united rival ethnic, tribal and credal forces. While it might have had a psychological need to 'divide and rule' it had a stronger practical need to 'unite and rule'. With the collapse of empires and the emergence of indigenous rulers, Third World politics become a force in its own right, eternally moralising in the United Nations and plausibly calling on the richer nations to surrender at least one per cent of their gross national product to reduce the gap between rich and poor. That a tepid response has come from the First World is partly to be explained by ingrained greed and obsession with its own economic problems. But there are other reasons. Left to their own devices, too many of the ex-colonies have dissolved into factionalism and sectionalism, tribalism and separatism. Government has fallen into the hands of restored hereditary privilegentsias, rapacious colonels or predatory bureaucrats whose capacity for syphoning off foreign aid would be envied by any bogus charity in the West. Bright young men go overseas not to study engineering, agriculture, medicine or any of the other basic skills on which the future of their countries depends, but law, politics or some other avenue to personal enrichment. When they have gained their just reward they too will join the chorus of international sloganeers inveighing against extremes of rich and poor nations while, in their own, riches and poverty have never been more divergent, or against discrimination against racial minorities in the First World while, in the Third, such minorities are being butchered. It is not perhaps surprising that, confronted with mediocracies in many emergent nations that make those in the developed nations look honest and honourable by comparison, the latters' taxpayers are increasingly loath to dig deeply into their pockets. Yet without that digging the world remains dangerously unbalanced and unjust – and potentially explosive.

Disturbed by power blocs wherever and however they arose, men of good will looked hopefully, or prayerfully, towards the 'non-aligned' nations as custodians of the world's conscience and powerhouse for its peace movement. Soon, however, these nations were strangled by slipping haloes. In defence of what were held to be vital national interests they were as bellicose as anyone else, while their internal politics did not display that socialist fraternity or *guru* goodness which they never tired of advertising. One of them was indicted for 'further restrictions of academic freedom and violations of the United Nations Charter on Human Rights',[1] another for perpetuating 'close links with the past with all that it means in superstition and obscurantism' and 'bloody riots'.[2] Cynicism over the non-aligned nations is no justification of militarism, but does nothing to encourage disarmament. Only exceptional leadership could have succeeded in any case, for 'the fact is that nuclear disarmament is not only most unlikely, it is virtually impossible. The reason for this is that in any disarmament situation, you could never be assured that your opponent had destroyed all his stocks of weapons. . . . Nuclear weapons are quite small and are easy to conceal.'[3]

When Tennyson wrote of 'the Parliament of Man, the Feder-

---

1 'An Open Letter to President Tito' by fourteen overseas professors in *New Humanist*, March 1974.
2 A. B. Shah, 'Obscure and Degrading', in *New Humanist*, April 1974.
3 Sir Philip Baxter, 'Nuclear realities', in the (Sydney) *Sun-Herald*, 7 October 1973.

ation of the world,'[1] he was thinking of an assembly of merito-crats wisely and disinterestedly directing the affairs of nations to universal satisfaction. With the establishment first of the League of Nations, then of the United Nations, it looked as if such an assembly might be at the prototype stage. While good work has been done through international agencies co-ordinating action in such fields as communications, banking, health, meteorology and insect control, the grand design of world government is still a design but looks less grand. Most nations are unhappy enough under their own mediocracies without seeking subservience to a lowest common multiple of international mediocracies. Yet who would be optimistic enough to think it can be avoided? On a globe of diminishing distances, why should the rise of the mediocracy, which is an international phenomenon, be restricted to political nationalism?

[1] *Locksley Hall*, London, 1842, 1.128.

CHAPTER SEVENTEEN

Rancid Research

'The masters of scientific patronage are less able to recognise the quality of research than the quantity of claims for it.... The successful researcher... needs the salesman's gift for mixing drinks and self-advertisement.... Mumbo-jumbo gains an academic status, albeit restricted, while anti-mumbo-jumbo has none.'

With the decline and fall of the intellectual has come an unfavourable climate for all intellectual pursuits. Among them is – or was – research. As the broad picture of the universe slides into focus, new knowledge comes from directing institutional telescopes at an infinity of intervening gaps. Induction and deduction, inspired guesses and relentless calculation continue to play their part, but conceptualising is liable to get lost in a plethora of minute observations and mathematical formulae. With instruments so refined that natural phenomena and artifacts defy separation, research 'findings' are increasingly arbitrary and disputation has become endemic. Battles are fought with an abandon stemming from bored frustration, like the scurry of an anthill in a desert of dust. The problem of bigness has multiplied and divided specialisation. It has flooded printing presses with an ocean of trivial and often erroneous observations that it is impossible for any one brain to navigate or any one pocket to filter. It has put the practical researcher and the director of research ever farther apart and entrusted to the luck of committees what had once been the skill of an individual.

Through rarefied instrumentation to observe and computerisation to collate, research faces mounting bills that only governments or multinational corporations can readily meet. The result is that, in every sense, it has become less 'pure'. It is impossible to predict not only what conclusions will be reached but how they will be applied, so that moral responsibility grows as remote as conceptual integration and both eventually disappear. Like the private in a war whose origins elude him, the scientist protests that he is only doing his job, that technological horror is not of his hatching. Since important research findings are likely to have either military implications or commercial potential of unprecedented size, and as military espionage and industrial espionage rank highly among contemporary professions or enterprises, 'security' is as essential to many research institutes as electricity. Even where it is not a matter of safeguarding millions (in men or money) security has become an obsession. The least, as well as the most, sensitive area is choked with it. Freely disseminating one's discoveries for the benefit of mankind is less important to the successful researcher than carefully timed and attributed publication on which may hang, if not the fate of nations, the offer of university chairs or the availability of further research funds. For the masters of scientific patronage are less able to recognise the quality of research than the quantity of claims for it.

Unless there were some immediate military or commercial objectives, research might readily get lost in a wilderness of false trails. Yet it is not always easy to define such objectives. To keep large staffs employed and big funds flowing, therefore, neophilia is consulted. It is usually able to give a trendy answer to the question of incentive. If uncertain what is relevant or significant, neglected or necessary – criteria on which research decisions were once reached – the ambitious researcher has only to follow fashion.

> Some sectors of scientific research are sexy, some are not; and therein lies one of the basic problems in trying to manage a nation's research and development effort. ... Rothschild discovered whole areas of sickness – mental illness, rheumatism, arthritis, dental caries and others – that the Medical Research Council saw as unsexy and largely ignored. He used as his yardstick of research relevance the occupancy of hospital beds in Britain – and found no correlation between that and the research council's programme.[1]

[1] David Fishlock, 'The sexy areas of scientific research aren't the needed ones', in *The Australian Financial Review*, 21 November 1973.

The successful researcher is now type-cast. To be able to control programmes and, above all, ensure that his name is attached to anything worthwhile that flows from them, he will need a position of power. To have reached that pinnacle he will have many talents: those of politician, salesman, bureaucrat. He must glory in politicking as budgets are determined and rivals are toppled. His love for security procedures must rival that of a counter-espionage agent. He needs the salesman's gift for mixing drinks and self-advertisement. If he ever had broad vision, intellectual objectivity or moral scruples, he shed them a long way down the ladder. If his party or religious allegiance is not impeccable, it must not be peculiar. Sometimes it is better to hold wrong views quietly than right views noisily. Academic brilliance or creative genius is not expected – and rarely offered.

Under the guidance of this mediocracy research has taken a number of characteristic turns. It has responded to the rise of democracy with the rise of sociology – an area without rigorous academic standards and a perfect tabernacle for enshrining popular myths and trendy divinities. A similar concern has undercut research in other subjects, for example, social Darwinism, eugenics and classics. Yet popularity or 'relevance' has made little impact on the PhD thesis, which is as likely to be of arcane obscurity as of bland banality, dressing up the incredible or the obvious in drapes of figures or formulae which give it a spurious dignity. These theses, and books based on them, are often extended bibliographies, or bibliographies of bibliographies. Especially in literature and philosophy, commentaries are more fashionable than aesthetic or normative statements, and comments on commentaries most fashionable of all. Even this jejune material is able to provoke the full hostilities of internecine research, but with words losing their precise meanings the rocket fire is random and casualties are few.

However given to neophilia, research establishments, especially in the academic world, may seek a respectable foundation. Outside certain halls of learning that have carved out a market for themselves in idiosyncratic studies, work that is less respectable may languish.

These PK [psychokinesis] effects are being demonstrated by experimenters who have chosen to work in the fringe field of parapsychology. It is almost impossible to get finance for this kind of research; experiments are long and often very tedious, results are meagre and difficult to publish, and scorn is plentiful and easy to find.[1]

Perhaps. But if fringe fields find it 'almost impossible to get finance', studies in refutation find it quite impossible. Certain research institutes specialise in the fringe. It may be through the special interests of their directors; it may be their mediocrity is so commanding they fear investigations more demanding. Once committed, they rarely concede mistakes. Bigger, more prestigious places, on the other hand, decline to investigate what 'everyone knows to be false'. Moreover, to demonstrate inadequacy among academic colleagues, however misguided, or fraud among their subjects would not be good publicity for a system greedy for research funds and fearful lest its sheep might starve with its goats. So mumbo-jumbo gains an academic status, albeit restricted, while anti-mumbo-jumbo has none. Eventually large numbers of the half-educated – a breed that has grown with the rise of mediocrity – believe to be true what 'everyone knows to be false'.

Outside the fringe fields one may find tendentious research. Old manuscripts relating to biblical times and likely to cast doubt on religious orthodoxy are appropriated, translated and interpreted by fraternities that have some interest in proving them innocuous to faith. This is a continuation of times when religion was the sole province of religious. Religion was then, however, relevant to the lives of ordinary people. Today it is not. Yet the more it is redundant the more it is researched.

[1] Lyall Watson, *Supernature: The Natural History of the Supernatural* London, 1973, p. 166.

CHAPTER EIGHTEEN

Expendable Education

'Education has been made universal and compulsory without regard to its social relevance, academic standards or cost. . . . The hapless child becomes the illiterate and innumerate victim of warring, ego-tripping academic factions.'

Perhaps the best portent for continued rise of the mediocracy, and one that promises to turn an atmospheric into a meteoric ascent, is the state of education from the nursery to the university, the classroom to the ministry. Educational meritocrats of a hundred years ago sought to blend the best of the past with the best of the present. Educational mediocrats of today have managed to inject the worst of the present into the worst of the past. Thus education upholds hereditary privilegentsias, redundant religion and absurd traditions while fomenting the collapse of authority, the rise of bureaucracy, the problem of bigness, the decline and fall of liberalism and the intellectual, and a whole encyclopaedia of philias.

Virtually throughout the world education has been made universal and compulsory without regard to its social relevance, academic standards or cost. Even more than happens with vacuum-cleaners, the education industry remorselessly expands in utter disregard of its quality and utter absolution from self-justification. Radical chic has so conditioned taxpayers and rate-payers to the concept that education is 'a good thing' that no one who does not want to be branded as a 'fascist pig' dares to oppose the steady raising of the school leaving age (which is so well-entrenched it has gained acronym status as RSLA) and proliferation of universities, when whatever gives education meaning is disintegrating. Until recent years there was lively academic debate over whether 'education' should enshrine the values of *educare* (to instruct) or *educere* (to lead out). Today the notion of values, as distinct from traditions, is alien to the Right; while both values and traditions are anathema to the Left.

In the schools a sickly authoritarianism struggles in the face of a breakdown of communications and discipline, imposed or self-generated. Headteachers exult in Pyrrhic victories over hair length, attire, staffroom revolts and attempted debate by pupils of fundamental educational problems, while the school fabric is torn apart and the ordinary teacher is exhausted or driven to breakdown or resignation by the sheer effort of preserving semi-silence or maintaining self-defence. From the sanctuary of ever remoter studies in ever vaster institutions, principals exercise one of their only two talents – the other is commanding the political influence that secured their appointment – a facility in writing reports which conceal the true state of violence and vandalism and save administrators from public protest. Wilful wastage of equipment and material by bad pupils is also concealed by curtailing supplies to good ones. 'Keep them amused' and 'don't see them smoking in the toilets' are the only instructions senior teachers give to junior ones. As the most cynical teachers grasp the numerous prizes of departmental headships, special responsibility and other allowances, and as the school community settles to the level of the laziest, loudest and most loutish of its pupils, the cream of the staff flees to private schools. Since many pupils perform the service of advising their teachers, who not infrequently have limited and idealistic notions of the world, that their unskilled and uneducated parents are earning more money than their pedagogues, a growing percentage of staff leaves the 'profession' altogether. Already understaffed schools are further depleted of childminders just as politicians, bureaucrats and principals magnify their status and incomes by expanding the school population through RSLA. Rebellious teenagers, maturing earlier both physically and sexually year by year, caged in buildings that would in many cases be condemned were they private factories or offices, conscious that they are earning and learning nothing where they are, are suddenly required to waste another year there.

In the nineteenth century the bulk of those educated at all left school at eleven with a firm grounding in the three Rs and a smattering of whatever else might appear on a limited syllabus. In today's superschools the syllabus is as long and complicated as a weekend racing guide, and a large and mounting percentage of pupils leaves school at sixteen completely illiterate. This situation is attributable to both the teaching atmosphere in the secondary school and innovation in the primary. As basic education sinks into an academic slime, pundits and experimenters pop up like bubbles with new formulae for painless input of knowledge. Switched ceaselessly from dictionary to phonetic alphabets, ideograms to 'look and say' words, mathematical tables to algebraic concepts, and all in the name of progress, simplicity, accelerated development and 'child-centred' education, the hapless child becomes the illiterate and innumerate victim of warring, ego-tripping academic factions who neither know nor care that the greatest obstacle to learning is not 'wrong' teaching methods but no teaching method at all. They are also unaware or heedless that the greatest obstacle to moral development is social instability.

Even the most placid of the mediocrats are dimly conscious that all is not well, that academic subjects do not seem to be appreciated by non-academic pupils, that the student body is dissatisfied. That the morale of abler members of staff is at a nadir is not an item that mediocracies record; they expect it. If resignations result, life will be easier. Basic problems are not as irritating as protest against them. When only mediocrities remain, protest will be minimal. Besides, they have remedies. If examinations are a nuisance, abolish them. Pupils will then be spared the 'trauma of failure' and the world spared the artificiality of once-for-all achievement. Or if exams are to be held, all the textbooks should be made available. Learning by rote is *passé*, school reports on general 'ability' are 'in'. The result is that limited (even after unwarranted expansion of) university places are filled by the pupils of schools sufficiently venal or ideological or self-seeking to puff reports, and are lost to pupils whose head-teacher or form teacher has a knife in them; while the labour market is flooded with recruits who were never when young required to exercise intellectual or moral discipline or practise concentration. So secretaries spend their working lives looking up dictionaries for simple words they never learnt to spell, clerks feeding electronic calculators with simple sums they never learnt to do, and professional men deferring decisions till they can locate in textbooks simple information they never bothered to learn. If pupils are bored with subjects they find, often with justification, irrelevant to their lives as individuals and future citizens, parents and breadwinners, mediocracy does not think of giving sex education, basic politics and economics, do-it-yourself classes and other relevant courses, but magnifies disruption with 'free periods', 'options' and amorphous 'leisure'. Some of these devices have come in from 'progressive' schools where, with small classes, exceptional teachers and caring parents, they may work well. In an already unstable situation they only increase instability.

Tertiary education may minister to a substantial number of reluctant students, especially in the first year, following the whims of parents or employers or headteachers rather than their own decisions, but they usually 'drop out' in the middle of their courses and are not like the conscripts one finds at the primary or secondary level. In the lower reaches of technical colleges apprentices on 'day release' may cause similar problems of in-discipline and disruption to those that flourish in secondary schools, but increasingly it is political 'consciousness' that is turning universities from their ordinary work. Proclaiming that student years are times for 'experimentation' and that the younger generation has insights denied its elders, undergraduates have turned campuses into arenas of drearily derivative sloganeering and – with able assistance from insensitive adminis-trations and trigger-happy police – battlefields. Young people unable to run a student society with a budget of hundreds believe they have a mission to run the university itself with a budget of millions. Instead of producing essays and projects they produce – according to temperament – rifles, 'sit-ins', oriental 'thoughts' or flowers, while examination papers that do not fire their candi-dates are fired by them. Yet when the time of expected gradu-ation approaches, 'progressive' students prove no more idealistic and disinterested than reactionaries. For the Left knows as well as the Right that while a degree may tell little about individual knowledge or talents and less about political commitment or human worth, it is an excellent meal-ticket or passport to special increments for the rest of one's life. Or, rather, it used to be. As the mediocracy has risen higher in education than in some other fields, the employment world is less inclined than in the past to offer glittering jobs and sparkling pay-packets commensurate with what graduates deem their right; and a main result of the university explosion is the creation of an 'intellectual proletariat', unemployed or unemployable, uncreative and discontented, fulfilled only on returning to campus to activate more student protest.

For the disintegration of universities their faculties may be indicted if not as accomplices then as accessories before the fact. Some of them are openly contemptuous of the academic values they are supposedly sustaining. Even in the profession of 'revolution' they are, for the most part, so narrow in knowledge, shallow in analysis and short in sincerity that they are incapable of inspiring a new society or any sort of society at all. At the other end of senior common rooms are professors and lecturers so engrossed in spilling 'publish or perish' articles into technical journals, flooding the book market with paperback popularisers or swelling the air waves with alternating jeremiads and instant solutions, they have no time or interest left for their students. So successful are they at clandestine politicising they manage to pose as apolitical. Torn between the Left and the Right, 'disciplines' like sociology and law, economics and politics, have fragmented on purely political lines where they have managed to escape disintegration from rancid research. Only in launching gamesmanship and oneupmanship, deadwood and driftwood, are students allowed to participate. Creative involvement would not suit the mediocracy.

Nothing has more confirmed the decline and fall of liberalism and the intellectual than their fate in universities. Here it is, as one academic owns,

> *de rigueur* to cultivate a certain mediocrity, not only in dress and manners but also in performance, since it is very bad form indeed to be an outstanding or popular teacher.... I felt that many of my friends had remained, intellectually and spiritually, exactly where I had left them; that students showed little thirst for knowledge; ... and that the academic world, at least in the sphere of my own interests, was a tower of decaying ivory.[1]

It may be a tower of élitism. It has nothing to do with meritocracy.

[1] Alan Watts, *In My Own Way*, pp. 220 and 335.

CHAPTER NINETEEN

Poisoned Professions

'Most intelligent laymen have grown tired of hiring professionals only to do the bulk of their job for them. . . . Though the radical chic attribute our economic woes to a chaos of unplanned, unprofessional growth, economic planning and "professionalism" have never been more dominant.'

Infected education has managed to poison the other professions. Despite the information explosion in all of them, their academic credentials and professional credibility have never looked shakier. Partly they are innocent victims of a trendy contempt for those who represent in theory, if not in practice, obsolescent traditions of apprenticeship, diligence, dedication and intellectual brilliance. Because these traditions are not entirely dead and, in support of claims for better pay and conditions, they hesitate to brandish the strike weapon as recklessly as do workers in power, transport and other essential industries on which human lives ultimately depend, they have also incurred general contempt by losing at most levels the economic differential which once marked them off from the general run of non-professionals. Indeed, in many cases they now earn considerably less than skilled or semi-skilled workers, and about as much as unskilled labourers, in key enterprises. But much of the fate of the professions may be attributed to mediocracies which have risen to the top of them and stifled professional values with trendiness, politicising, bureaucracy and bungling. A number of professions warrant brief attention as they not only contribute to the social picture but are significant in their own right. The second-oldest profession has already been considered; the oldest and hitherto one of the most valuable has in most countries now been declared illegal by mediocratic Puritans. Once the oldest profession was an extension of the second-oldest; now it is an extension of the underworld. But just as most intelligent laymen have grown tired of hiring professionals only to do the bulk of their job for them, so young people at least are finding the permissive society has made the oldest profession as redundant as the second-oldest.

Among the 'useful' professions law is probably the most poisoned. If Justice Shallow is any indication, it was not held in particularly high esteem in Shakespeare's England, but it took the heavy involvement of lawyers in the French Revolution and the Reign of Terror to demonstrate to the world at large that the profession whose job it is to uphold the law is that which holds it in the greatest contempt. The Russian Revolution is one of the many subsequent upheavals where the same fact has been demonstrated, and in our own day leading lawyers have played a dominant role in the collapse of the world's most powerful Executive through alleged involvement in corruption, perjury, conspiracy, tax evasion, bribery, blackmail and perversion of justice. Corporation lawyers are among the slickest operators in multinational companies, every shady firm – and sometimes it seems there are more that are shady than sunny – has a twilight attorney on the board or in the wings, and solicitors' 'trust' funds stand a fair chance of finishing up with their guardians in a country without extradition treaties or traceable banking accounts. Yet the profession is the most pious and moralistic outside holy orders, tireless in urging 'law and order' on permissive societies, in processing to churches for the opening of law terms and in filling courtrooms with Bibles instead of affirmation cards. As if to make amends for its revolutionary fringe it is, on the whole, rooted in deep conservatism. While its support of the traditions of common law is a valuable bulwark against instability and neophilia, it also supports a number of traditions valueless save to hereditary privilegentsias.

If some lawyers have shown a social conscience and liberal outlook it has been, for the most part, in defiance of the mediocracy of the profession. Much of the time of its members is devoted to word-spinning in legal complexity and trivia of its own creation. Once it was said that the law, like the Ritz Hotel, was open to rich and poor alike. Now, with Legal Aid, only the very rich and the very poor can face the economics of legal entanglement with equanimity. For middle-income groups, win or

lose their case, it is a financial disaster. Through their appearance and accent, if not through the quality of counsel allotted
them, the very poor are still likely to gain the least satisfactory
outcome from judges and magistrates inherently suspicious of the
lower orders. So the situation has arisen that more people fear
being taken down by lawyers than by those acknowledged
vultures and conmen who increasingly thrive in complex modern
society. This complexity has come about through the rise of
bureaucracy and technology and the problem of bigness, with a
growing intrusion of government into the lives of individuals and
voluntary societies, the proliferation of regulations in efforts to
control the hazards of new industrial processes and forms of
transport, and the mushrooming of administrative law to inter-
relate the parts of increasingly fragmented society. As the
ordinary citizen has little time to study this growing complexity,
and may never be personally involved in the operations of a
battery of tribunals and commissions funded by big government,
many of the profession's mediocrities flourish without criticism.
In more conventional courts and the routine of solicitors'
practices, however, lawyers are feared as much for their incompetence as for their corruption. Great nineteenth-century
meritocrats like Charles Bradlaugh showed how able, active and
single-minded laymen could trounce the professionals, and
mounting costs have induced voluntary organisations today to
prepare 'kits' for lay conveyancing and applications for divorce.
That more people do not use them is not a token of confidence in
the legal profession but of a soundly-based belief that as town
clerks and responsible civil servants in legal departments of
public instrumentalities are usually, and judges always, lawyers
themselves, it pays to be represented by other lawyers. For the
same reasons of mediocratic solidarity, laymen hesitate to take
lawyers to law and the profession is largely free of internal purging or even self-criticism.

Though it has less opportunity for fraud and less taste for
politics, the medical profession does not enjoy much more esteem
than the legal. It, too, has been invaded by the rise of bureaucracy and technology and vexed by the problem of bigness. It, too,
has an establishment of ultra-conservatism and, especially in
psychiatry, a lunatic fringe. Above all, the mystique of professional dedication and financial disinterest which it enjoyed when
doctors came from a class in society with private means, has all
but vanished. That they have suffered less than other profes-

sional groups in the decline and fall of the intellectual is largely to be explained by their gift throughout the twentieth century of keeping a stethoscope to the business pulse, and a microscope to the main chance, of the community. While junior hospital doctors often work punishingly and impecuniously, medical mediocrities can amass great fortunes by specialising in abortions, legal or illegal, or 'cashectomies' (needless, easy and profitable operations) and by acquiring shares in private nursing homes or treating the neuroses of the wealthy. Lust for money has compounded an 'engineering' approach to medicine that has accompanied the rise of technology and led to the neglect of preventive medicine. Outside the dubious world of psychoanalysis, which can explain everything, charge anything and cure nothing that could not be treated more simply by other means, psychiatry has pursued drug and shock therapy at the expense of social and psychological understanding. So insensitive to the human situation of his patients is the average psychiatrist that irrational reactions flourish among professional rebels and disillusioned laymen alike. One group proclaims that even psychotics are saner than their doctors, while the other provides a ready market for bogus cults that advertise hostility to psychiatry with promises of 'control over self'.

The 'engineering' approach of modern medicine has had many consequences. It has put 'miracle cures' before medical care, promoted gadgetry at any price, encouraged animal and human experiments of doubtful value, fired a 'rat race' among pharmaceutical companies from which tragedies like thalidomide babies have sprung, and turned patients into pillboxes. 'Therapeutic' addiction to tranquillisers, sedatives and stimulants, to say nothing of cosmetic therapy for 'unsightly fat' or 'sluggish systems', is the real 'drug problem' of contemporary society. It has arisen partly in response to patient demand resulting from the semi-educated reading the semi-factual in semi-serious magazines and paperbacks, partly because it is easier and more profitable for a doctor to treat symptoms chemically than find causes in the personal or familial history of patients. Through 'ethical' advertising medicine has become an extension of admass and through media sensationalism an extension of showbiz. Certain 'sexy' subjects like heart transplant operations and cardiac intensive care units command human and financial resources out of all proportion to achievement. An artificial heart valve or convalescence at home may work as well as these very expensive undertakings. Those who '...strive/Officiously to keep alive'[1] may come to believe, if they did not always believe, that patients exist for the good of research and not conversely. Thus hospitals are becoming ever vaster and more impersonal and patients, especially in poorer districts, are dying because there are no local hospitals or general practitioners to look after them before they can be transferred to medical factories of modest effectiveness and insatiable urge to pump in unnecessary sedatives and antibiotics.

Like lawyers, doctors are increasingly but vainly questioned on whether they do what they should, omit what they should avoid, or do competently what they attempt. It is said they bury their mistakes. They also bury recollection of their colleagues' incompetence, so that in most countries it is more difficult to redress medical than legal wrongs. It has become conventional to pay tribute to the marvels of modern medicine, but new investigations are less comforting. Man, it is said, had relatively little infectious or degenerative disease when he was a primitive hunter-gatherer of food. With the unbalanced diet and unhealthy homes of a settled agricultural way of life, both types of disease spread. Industrial societies reduced infection less by antibiotics and immunisation than by improving diets and sanitation, but greatly added to degenerative conditions caused by smoking, air pollution, noise, tension and other circumstances of modern life. In recent years there appears to have been a levelling off – and for some social and age groups a fall – of hitherto rising life expectancy, while old age seems to be a time of growing illness, neglect and loneliness. It is understandable that general practitioners should resent being paid less to call to mend a patient's body than a plumber to mend his pipes, but their expectation of human gratitude is out of proportion to their mediocratic deserts.

In a materialistic age fewer people agonise over the state of their health than over the state of their finances. This anxiety stems not from the machinations of *laissez-faire* capitalism, which is dead or dying, but from the functioning of fiscal systems and investment outlets overseen by economists, accountants, stockbrokers, consultants and other professional groups in the bureaucracy, big institutions and accredited institutes. Though the radical chic attribute our economic woes to a chaos of unplanned, unprofessional growth, economic planning and 'pro-

1 Arthur Clough, *The Latest Decalogue*, London and Cambridge, 1862, lines 11–12.

fessionalism' have never been more dominant. Most basic of the professions in the financial field is economics. Indeed, so trendy is it that it has taken over from the classics as the basic training of the administrative class and *literati* generally. The classics, it is said, was about a dead world; economics is about a live one. However plausible this may seem in theory, practice is very different. Study of the classics gave insight into the architectonics of modern languages and fostered clarity and brevity of expression. It also fostered humanistic and cultural values by concentrating on a segment of world history after the dark ages of pagan ignorance and before the Dark Ages of religious obscurantism. And it was about a real world. In the form of econometrics, economics is increasingly invaded by the unreal world of mathematics. A plethora of mathematical symbols and logical chains related to input-output matrices, multiplier effects and technical micro-analysis are not only a distraction from real issues like supply, demand and distribution but pretend to an exactitude of economic calculation which is impossible even if all variables have been taken into consideration. And when all schools of economics – classical, Marxist, Keynesian and monetarist – and innumerable sub-schools and eclectic variants have notoriously failed to recognise psychological and political factors staring them in the face, not to mention technological potential that is always out of sight, economists usually ignore the most vital variables. Unfortunately, at an impressionable age managers, bureaucrats and politicians come to accept this phantasy world as reality and base their investment, fiscal and monetary policies on its projections. Sectional greed and rampant nationalism do not assist wise and equitable planning nationally or internationally, but the world's currency crises, persistent poverty, wild alternations of inflation and stagnation (and now stagflation) and the co-existence of gluts and shortages are largely the creation of a growing band of feuding, shortsighted and self-satisfied economic mediocrats.

Since the success of Keynesianism in dealing with 'under-heated' economies during the Great Depression, 'the orthodox theory, held with an almost religious devotion by the "authorities" (that is, the chief pundits in the financial and banking world as well as in the Treasury itself), had proved a good working rule' for 'overheated' economies too; but from 1962 'the traditional forms of febrifuge – bloodletting, purging and rest' failed to work.[1] With true mediocratic myopia, economists under-react to political crises and over-react to economic crises. They are single-minded when they ought to be open-minded and bird-brained when they ought to be single-minded.

If economists are architects for the grand design of economic disaster, accountants have proved trusty contractors. In their less intellectually demanding world they have managed to create not only rival schools of thought but rival professional bodies. Just as economists assess employment or balance of payments or wholesale price levels within days of the release of figures showing a contrary situation, so auditors repeatedly manage to aver that glowing company books present a 'true and fair' view of a firm's financial affairs within days of its going into liquidation. But whereas economists – unless they are seen to be making a great fortune from potboiling punditry – are generally assumed to be honest, however aberrant their conclusions, accountants have gained a reputation for integrity approaching that of lawyers. Corporation accountants have proved almost as slick operators as corporation lawyers in multinational companies, and resting beside a twilight attorney in every shady firm there always seems to be a dusky accountant. While exercising a great gift for exegesis of double-entry accounting and nitpicking proficiency in detecting tiny discrepancies in petty-cash books, the profession is adept at concealing the actual state of a company from its shareholders, if not from its directors.

In the great bulk of cases, however, as one would expect of a mediocracy, concealment is unintentional and the firm's auditors are as uncomprehending as its shareholders and perhaps as its directors, its accountants and – if it employs them – its actuaries. Company accounts demonstrate everything but the true value of assets, current liquidity, entanglement with 'associated' companies (where there are interlocking directorships) and future profitability. Lacking an audited budget of future operations or a clear statement of present affairs, shareholders and creditors have only a picture of antiquarian interest. Accounts rarely show the true appreciation of property and true depreciation of plant. In times of inflation they are still linked to historical cost and not constant-purchasing-power cost, to first-in-first-out instead of last-in-first-out inventory accounting, to fixed rather than floating exchange rates. Thus, for the most part, they are presenting an inflated level of pre-tax profits on which

[1] Harold Macmillan, *At the End of the Day*, pp. 84 and 85.

tax is paid and union demands calculated. The result is that actual return on capital from equity investment is diminishing all the time, which is one of the reasons for institutional disfavour.

In the community at large accountants are in no better odour. Radical-chic expectations that they should report on the social aims and environmental impact of company operations go unreasonably beyond their professional competence; but there is widespread suspicion that the ablest accountancy brains are syphoned off from welfare programmes and productivity drives into the lucratively parasitic field of income tax avoidance by wealthy clients.

Stockbrokers are, perhaps, in worse odour than accountants. Indeed, so unpopular are they and the markets they represent, that theirs is one of the few mediocracies rising only in terms of mediocrity, not of numbers. Its redundancy is recognised. If asked for their advice on particular investments, brokers are wont to say that if they knew the answer they would not be brokers but share traders. Many of them are, in fact, not only share traders but company promoters and new-issue underwriters, off-loading unwanted shares on to, and prising deflated shares away from, their clients. The failure rate of broking firms demonstrates that even at this operation a fair percentage is inefficient. But if they are regarded solely as commissioned agents, their declining capacity to execute orders accurately or promptly calls their basic function into question. Already the bulk of successful companies borrow far in excess of their paid-up capital and usually through the money market, not the stock-market. If 'capital' could not be entirely replaced by mortgages, secured loans and statutory declarations by directors, stock-brokers could surely be replaced by an equity totalisator.

For every broker who is productive, two are counter-productive. Serviced by a batch of chartists and analysts thrown up by the rise of sociology and exchanging misinformation with a team of financial journalists, who are usually unqualified both professionally and conceptually, they never tire of dispensing in general what they are too coy to impart in particular. Through regular circulars and off-the-cuff forecasts of bandwagon originality they unduly inflate bull markets and depress bear ones, thus adding to the neurosis and 'future shock' of society. Big pension funds, insurance companies and other institutional investors who make their own decisions take advantage of the fact that brokers induce small investors to sell when they should buy and buy

when they should sell. As a profession brokers have few
theoretical, and fewer practical, requirements. As an industry
they apparently have no notion of their return on capital. As a
hereditary privilegentsia they needlessly exacerbate the 'class
struggle'. If the 'stockbroker belts' of metropolitan fringes have
to be renamed, few will weep at the rededication ceremony.

Throughout the professional world – which has continued to
expand despite the decline and fall of the intellectual – the 'love'
of amateurs has been replaced by the supposed detachment of
professionals. It is true that in social work continuous and informed support is better than sporadic do-goodism. It is also true
that 'professionalism' has often become associated with the
slavish execution of certain 'techniques' devoid of insight or foresight. This is especially found in professions connected with
'social engineering'. Psychology has become 'overpragmatic, over-
Puritan, and overpurposeful'.[1] Quantification is all-important;
the human subject has become the human object. From the end
of the nineteenth century 'psychology was in a sense depersonal-
ised; self-scrutiny and the examination, study and analysis of
others' motivation were discredited as the methodological core of
the discipline.'[2]

Through its triumph 'the statistically normal mind is accepted
as being synonymous with the psychologically healthy mind'.[3]

> The truth which the informed are hesitant to reveal and the
> uninformed are amazed to discover is that academic psych-
> ology has contributed nothing to the knowledge of human
> nature. It has not only failed to bring to light the great,
> hauntingly recurrent problems, but it has no intention, one is
> shocked to realize, of attempting to investigate them.[4]

From this attitude most of mainstream psychiatry and 'psycho-
technology' is derived. Though dominated by current defeatism
and an unimaginative mediocrity, 'the psychological and social
sciences must enable us to control the animalistic, barbaric, and
primitive propensities in man'.[5] While claiming to illuminate the

[1] Abraham Maslow, *Motivation and Personality*, New York, 1954, p. 291.
[2] Gregory Rochlin, *Man's Aggression: The Defence of the Self*, Boston, 1973,
pp. 54–5.
[3] Wilfred Trotter, *Instincts of the Herd in Peace and War*, London, 1916,
pp. 78–9.
[4] Henry Murray, 'Psychology and the University', in *Archives of Neurology
and Psychology*, CXXXIV (1935), 805.
[5] Kenneth B. Clark, 'The Pathos of Power: A Psychological Perspective', in
American Psychologist, XXVI (December 1971), 1047.

great, hauntingly recurrent problems of mankind, psychoanalysis miserably 'begins from the mystical assertion that the psycho-sexual energy of the unconscious is a blind and stupid outrush of pure lust'.[1] Happily, psychoanalysis has had more impact on the impotent literary mediocracy than on the potent mediocracy of social planning.

In the nineteenth century outstanding archaeological and anthropological discoveries were made in Troy, Crete, Egypt and the Third World by amateurs, who frequently contributed large sums of their own money to their investigations. In the twentieth century archaeology and anthropology became the overwhelming preserve of professionals whose 'exciting' new discoveries, regularly aired in the media, have had less impact on basic understanding than on microchronology. Most recently of all, a return of the amateur, or shamateur, has eclipsed the professionals. This is a person of minimal knowledge and – till he writes up his 'findings' for the masses of semiliterates – cash, but with a shrewd appraisal of public appetite for the sensational, mystical, all-embracing and spurious. Just when it seemed nothing could restore confidence in the mushrooming world of poisoned professions, he has put a new lustre on professional standards.

[1] Alan Watts, *In My Own Way*, p. 355.

CHAPTER TWENTY

Bungled Business

'There is a systematic public relations campaign, connived at by both governments and businesses, to promote the second-best and second-rate. . . . Fortunes are to be made rather by the sinking of oil wells or building of housing estates on hitherto neglected acres than by the development of an epoch-making invention.'

If all they had to contend with were carping economists, incompetent accountants and shifty stockbrokers, commerce and industry might do quite well. They are, however, squeezed by broader mediocratic forces, both internal and external.

Most pervasive and unpredictable is government. The excesses and inhumanity of *laissez-faire* capitalism made State intervention in business inevitable. Especially when this involves subsidies, tariff protection, export incentives and taxation 'holidays' most businessmen find it acceptable. Governments are expected to act as umpires, even to lay down the rules of the game. What is unacceptable is the increasingly prevalent habit of governments of changing these rules in the middle of play. Neophilia, response to democratic pressures, panic in the face of fluctuating world conditions all combine to produce bewildering and often unpredictable changes in fiscal and monetary policy, involving such important elements as exchange rates, taxation, official interest rates and statutory reserve deposits, and in attitudes to full or partial nationalisation, which render forward planning very difficult and create a perpetual climate of uncertainty. Among the results are a great expenditure of time in political 'watching' and lobbying instead of improving business efficiency and a tendency to form multinational corporations to try to balance out the actions of individual governments.

With their increasing size companies are facing not only a growth of external bureaucracy to keep an eye on them but of internal bureaucracy. Repeated mergers and takeovers that are supposed to produce 'economies of scale' are certainly creating the problem of bigness with poor communications, warring factions in the boardroom, bad public image and low staff morale. After a time these diseconomies of complexity may overcome the economies of scale, and 'blue chip' companies now tend to have poor returns on capital, low growth rates and no investment attractions as a hedge against inflation. To conserve, let alone increase, their savings investors are turning, especially in the short term, to non-labour-intensive industries. As one leading industrialist has bitterly commented, it is more profitable to manufacture 'money' than goods. In 'bull' markets, financial, property and mining 'exploration' shares, notably those massaged by 'funny money', do immeasurably better than leading industrials, and some of them do not do conspicuously worse in 'bear' markets. Consequently, the stockmarket looks more and more like a casino with the dice weighted and chips stacked against the 'outsider', whether it be an individual investor or a big institution which has not insisted on seats on the board.

Despite a growing tendency to bypass the stockmarket, a low market rating, which may not reflect a company's underlying strength, makes it more difficult to borrow from banks that still subscribe to the 'cult of the equity'. To preserve their cash flow, firms are tending to plough more of their profits into reserves, so that even in nominal value dividend disbursements in many countries have declined since the 1960s. Pension funds and insurance-assurance companies are thus finding it increasingly difficult in inflationary times to gain that return on equity investments which will guarantee the real value of pensions and policies when they mature. When inflation turns to hyperinflation the difficulty becomes an impossibility, with the result that individual saving is discouraged and people dread retirement. In seeking alternative investments, both individuals and institutions have turned to property, commodities, wine, art, antiques and manuscripts. The result is inflated values which are jeopardising the achievement of a property-owning democracy, making quality consumer goods prohibitively expensive and distorting cultural and intellectual standards.

Because they are politically sensitive the prices of basic food-stuffs and materials are sometimes kept at uneconomic levels, discouraging investment in them and encouraging investment in more rewarding luxuries and fripperies. While 'rising living standards' is a cant political phrase, there is a systematic public relations campaign, connived at by both governments and businesses, to promote the second-best and second-rate. Thus 'town houses' with poky gardens are made to sound more attractive than houses with worthwhile gardens but less attractive than 'luxury apartments' with no gardens at all. Peasant food with poor ingredients but trendy trimmings, flimsy plastic instead of durable wooden or metal products, synthetic fibres and every other form of inferior substitute is represented as being more fashionable than the original. To ensure continuity of consumption, 'planned obsolescence' has become a built-in feature of modern production and as big a contributor to worker alienation as the assembly-line itself. It also exaggerates the gap between the poor and the rich, who can still afford hand-crafted, custom-built, natural-product consumer goods.

Because of the mounting cost of the labour component of manufacturing, and the technological possibility of automation, unemployment is not regarded as the ill omen for business prospects and sharemarket prices that once it was. In the first phase of the Industrial Revolution booming business meant job opportunities and conversely; capitalists and wage slaves rejoiced or moaned together. Now the only thing which will help a jaded market is a good whiff of unemployment. In that sense, far from moderating with the rise of democracy, the 'class struggle' is more pronounced than ever. And one might be tempted to echo the Marxist cry of the irreconcilable contradictions of the capitalist system and the inevitability of socialism did the rise of bureaucracy and political anxiety not produce irreconcilable contradictions in the socialist countries. But perhaps the greatest economic difficulties are experienced by those two-party states where one party is socialist and the other anti-socialist; so that free enterprise is not free, nationalisation is not national, business uncertainty is maximal and morale in nationalised industries minimal.

In this atmosphere of uncertainty and unpredictability, where fortunes are to be made rather by the sinking of oil wells or building of housing estates on hitherto neglected acres than by the development of an epoch-making invention, mediocrities might be expected to have as good a chance of thriving as the most able. Other factors have led to an actual rise of mediocracy in business.

The founders of the great nineteenth-century industrial empires, like the merchant adventurers of earlier centuries, were entrepreneurs and men of vision. By their flair and good judgement, not to say ruthlessness, they created mass markets for chemicals, power, communications and processed foods. Their rivals overreached themselves and crashed; they nurtured personal savings and borrowings into great fortunes and enterprises for which they were personally responsible. Since their day these empires have mostly gone public. Their descendants have inherited their personal fortunes but not their personal responsibilities, or at least not sole responsibility. Many of them do not even trouble to occupy a somnolent seat on the board, and some have so little concern for the business whereby they live in affluence that they reside in distant tax havens or tourist resorts. A few are even known as 'angels' for revolutionary organisations, underground journals or sundry scheming hippies.

The firm's affairs are run by managerial bureaucrats who may initially know nothing about its products or processes, let alone the vision of its founder, but have supposed skills in 'management'. This reputation – which is a salable and often sold commodity, as executives tend increasingly to flit from firm to firm – is more likely to be lost by taking the wrong decision than by taking no decision at all. As they do not have ultimate control they are habitually terrified of being supplanted by someone below them in the hierarchy and tend to give more attention to business politics than to business policies. If they are elected to the board they join a happy band who may have few, if any, shares in the company but, while they remain directors, have virtually unlimited powers to vote themselves lush fringe benefits and emoluments (either directly or into wholly-owned 'management companies' incorporated in tax havens). These perquisites bear no direct relation to the success of the firm and, presumably, of their own efforts. Indeed there is often an inverse relation, since if the company seems to be 'on the skids' its directors are likely to snatch as much for themselves as they can before its creditors and shareholders are left to scrabble through the wreckage. If any attempt at all is made to answer really tricky questions before all is lost, they are probably referred to management consultants, who may well be failed or redundant businessmen.

There are, of course, still company directors who inject equity and personal effort into businesses they found, but since the establishment of joint-stock companies in the mid-nineteenth century this equity may be minimal.

> Some seven men form an Association
> (If possible, all Peers and Baronets),
> They start off with a public declaration
> To what extent they mean to pay their debts.
> That's called their Capital: if they are wary
> They will not quote it at a sum immense,
> The figure's immaterial – it may vary
> From 18 million down to 18 pence ...
> They then proceed to trade with all who'll trust 'em,
> Quite irrespective of their capital
> (It's shady, but it's sanctified by custom); ...
> If you succeed, your profits are stupendous –
> And if you fail – pop goes your 18 pence ...
> If you come to grief, and creditors are craving ...
> Do you suppose that signifies perdition?
> If so you're but a monetary dunce –
> You merely file a Winding-Up Petition,
> And start another Company at once![1]

The mediocratic revolution among employers is well mirrored by that among employees. Trade unionism for employees began in the nineteenth century in a climate of suppression and persecution. The early union leaders were men of outstanding moral courage, if not of ideological brilliance or organising genius. As the movement gained legal status and grudging acceptance before the working-class revolution set new social patterns, unionism supported, when it did not represent, many progressive causes: political emancipation, colonial justice, universal education, law reform and secularisation, together with concern for the health, compensation, job security and proper remuneration of workers. In the twentieth century we see a totally different movement. Able sons and grandsons of the older union leaders did not, for the most part, want to enter their fathers' and grandfathers' trades, and were able to secure education to enter the profes-

[1] W. S. Gilbert, *Utopia Limited; or, The Flowers of Progress*, London, 1893, Act I.

sional classes. Largely led by mediocrities and political time-servers, the unions grew obsessed with narrow industrial matters like wages and fringe benefits, left progressive causes to specialist bodies which were dominated by the middle classes, and might even oppose health and safety regulations if these seemed likely to reduce the earning potential of piece-workers.

With automation came the threat of massive unemployment and the promise of massive plenty. Instead of supporting an overall philosophy of planned work and leisure and a national (let alone an international) incomes policy, the powerful unions have insisted on closed shops, 'productivity deals' and blatant overmanning. These deals are made possible by technological innovations for which the workers were rarely responsible and against which, in some cases, they at first directed Luddite opposition. Automation is, moreover, possible only in certain industries, and work involving hand craftsmanship, personal service and intellectual effort cannot increase its 'productivity'. So we find the anomaly of compositors earning twice the income of senior reporters and up to twenty times the income of creative writers; of surplus employees with nothing to do earning more than harassed and overworked personnel in less fortunate industries; of strikes by key workers for 'productivity' awards depriving other workers of their productivity and even of their jobs or their lives (through reduced safety and the loss of winter heating). Poorly paid social-security workers are assaulted for not coping quickly enough with the demands of 'dependants' of striking, relatively well-paid workers for welfare payments from the community at large. Wages 'lost' by successful strikers are soon regained by retrospective awards or overtime to catch up on the backlog of work, while the financial loss and inconvenience suffered by other workers are never compensated for. Yet every strike is still hailed by the radical chic as a blow for 'freedom' against the government or the capitalist class as if no media mediocrat had ever noticed that cabinet ministers and tycoons travel in chauffeur-driven cars, have emergency power plants in their homes and are generally immune to the hazards of strikes. This cannot, of course, be pointed out without running the risk of being denounced as 'running dogs' or 'fascist pigs' or incurring boycott.

It is true that some strikes are justified today as in the nineteenth century. Whether justified or not, however, strikes have become an endemic and intractable feature of modern industry.

With ever-changing technology, 'demarcation' disputes are never-ending; with the collapse of authority, unofficial strikes would proliferate even if all official ones were to be abandoned; with the rise of democracy it is politically impossible outside totalitarian countries to operate effective sanctions against wilful breaking of industrial agreements. Strike-breaking is equally impossible. 'Owing to the greater interlocking and great complication of these plants, we cannot do what we did in the General Strike of 1926. We could produce little or quite insufficient power to meet the needs of a nation now wholly geared, industrially and domestically, to electricity.'[1] Mediocracy has become omnipotent.

[1] Harold Macmillan, *At the End of the Day*, p. 44.

F

CHAPTER TWENTY-ONE

Curbless Crime

'Police forces ... are assumed to be either in league with or stupider than crime syndicates. . . . As . . . pathetic little cases are processed through police stations and the courts, in the streets outside curbless crime of unquestioned virulence and arbitrary outbreak ravages the community.'

If criminals were geniuses and their syndicates omnipotent, it might be possible to speak of a rise of the meritocracy. Drawing distinctions between meritocracy and mediocracy is not necessarily to pass a moral judgement, though some critics suggest that the élitism of a meritocracy is frankly immoral. While certain of the mediocrats described in this book are obviously immoral, it does not seek to generalise about mediocracy at large from a moral standpoint. It does, however, assert that the nature of both crime and criminals in contemporary society favours mediocracy rather than meritocracy while, even when it seeks to curb crime, a mediocracy usually turns out to be impotent.

Theoretically, crime – however it be determined – has always been abhorrent to society. Those anarchists and communists who foresee a day when law will wither away are not 'easy on crime' but believe constituted authority fertilises rather than prunes it. Despite romanticised stories of Robin Hood and his Merry Men, Elizabethan Seadogs, highwaymen and bushrangers, criminals do not tend to be men with unconventional views on how to bring down tyrants and redistribute wealth, but are motivated by the narrowest self-interest. Unswerving loyalty is the main characteristic sought in colleagues. Though 'Mr Big' may be brilliant, thus escaping detection or at least conviction, he rarely favours a meritocracy. Someone who is suspicious of the world at large is often suspicious of his mates as well and feels safer when surrounded by nonentities. This element of suspicion, which promotes scheming against as well as scheming with one's associates, is found more in a mediocracy than in a meritocracy, criminal or otherwise. And, whatever may be true of the undetected white-collar criminal, those delinquents who are most conspicuous, cause most concern and engage most of the attention of law-enforcement agencies are not conspicuous for brains. Even if they are not, as is sometimes postulated, high-grade mental defectives, they are likely to be socially inadequate. Their criminality may come from alcoholism or drug addiction rather than any inherent incapacity to earn an honest living, but this syndrome is more likely to be the product of personality disorders than of hypersensitivity to the stupidity and rottenness of the world.

Those crimes which, by both their mounting incidence and their unpredictability, are most dreaded are violence against the person, whether beatings-up 'for kicks' or 'muggings' for trifling returns. They are making many men and most women afraid to go out at night in big cities and in some countries are turning blocks of luxury apartments into armed fortresses. It may be pointless to describe such crimes, which are clearly bringing some sort of satisfaction to the perpetrators, as 'irrational', but their cost effectiveness in terms of tangible benefits is minimal. And there is growing evidence that violence is a manifestation of an injured ego or the response of those who lack intellectual power or verbal facility for a non-violent retort. One group may be mediocre; the other, mediocre or worse.

The rise of democracy, universal education, social justice and professional police forces in the nineteenth century led to forecasts of the decline and fall of criminality. Crime, it was said, was caused by people's frustration at denial of political representation, lack of training in cultural appreciation or the means of livelihood, desperation in penniless adversity and low expectation of being caught. As these predisposing causes were swept away, crime would vanish with them. Unfortunately, the outcome has been opposite to the intention. Many people do not believe their individual votes have any impact and are more suspicious than ever of politics, which seems to them a better way of instituting or covering up than of preventing or tracking down crime.

Education has merely exposed impoverished teachers to the contemptuous gaze of delinquent children and allowed criminals to read about the techniques and rewards of crime. Social welfare has been a better boon to the wives of convicts than to the widows of their victims. Police forces are even more distrusted than politicians and are assumed to be either in league with or stupider than crime syndicates.

These are not the only reasons why crime has failed to decline and fall, why it has, on the contrary, so advanced with criminological and penological 'progress' that it seems to be beyond control. Political equality has given no boost to economic equality throughout modern society, though it has greatly encouraged expectations of this result. Unashamed advertising of luxuries forces on the attention of the poor knowledge of the things they are lacking, while the media demonstrate that people are listened to when they have money and power instead of conspicuous talent and glamorise violence as a means of achieving one's objectives. In a self-indulgent society material prosperity makes pressing demands and remorse is regarded as a sign of weakness. Penal reform has sometimes proved counter-productive. Suspending driving licences as an alternative to prison does not put delinquent motorists off the road but means that they drive unlicensed, uninsured, more nervously and at greater hazard to innocent road-users than before. Though some prisons are still disgracefully primitive, others have been so upgraded they are vastly better than the seedy religious hostels which are the only home deadbeat prisoners know outside.

Unattended displays in emporia and supermarkets seem to invite 'impulse' stealing, the extension of credit has increased the incidence of bouncing cheques and unpaid debts, and the high incomes that may be earnt by illiterate or backward people make them especially vulnerable to confidence tricks and outrageous, uncomprehended contracts. The rise of technology has made all merchandise more complicated for the layman and left him more open to misrepresentation, while it has put into criminal hands more lethal weapons and greater mobility. If the nefarious are still unlucky enough to be caught, one or other of the poisoned professions has already helped them to salt away their ill-gotten gains, the rise of sociology has made them news, and 'cheque-book journalism' offers a nice little nest-egg for 'telling all'.

Where criminal rewards are more substantial than fines, and suspended sentences, probation and parole common, it is not perhaps accurate to describe detection as a misfortune. Be that as it may, it is a hazard which largely applies to 'blue-collar' crime. 'White-collar' crooks rarely seem to be exposed. There is, however, evidence that this is a growth industry which might well be emulated by the generality of bungled business. Both motive and opportunity are responsible. In the modern world honest businessmen and professional men are not well remunerated for the worry, responsibility and unpaid overtime spent attending conferences, planning strategies and reading reports and trade and professional journals, that their work entails. Many factory supervisors and inspectors are paid substantially less than some of the men they are supervising or inspecting. Politicians earn less than pop stars and local politicians may get nothing but their expenses. The rise of bureaucracy has led to a mushrooming in every field of activity of officials, custodians, auditors, planners, quality controllers, contracting officers, insurance adjusters, inspectors, agents and buyers – to say nothing of policemen, customsmen and taxmen – whose modest incomes are out of proportion to those of wideboys who depend on their signatures or recommendations. Positions of this sort are prone to attract mediocrities or men whose talents flower only in an atmosphere of 'kickbacks' and corruption. Like the blossoming of defalcating lawyers, embezzling accountants, misrepresenting salesmen and other undergrowth of the affluent society, this florescence is fertilised by the problem of bigness, which makes it increasingly difficult to lay bare skulduggery. The ultimate in modern 'communications' – the computer – gives opportunities for fraud that have barely been considered. Once a bogus account is written into a computer's memory, exposure is very difficult as long as the account is operated in a statistically normal way.

Apart from the temptations to which individual police officers are exposed, law enforcement agencies suffer from many difficulties unforeseen by their founders over a century ago. Though efforts have been made to import the scientific revolution into police forces and organisations at risk, technology seems to be rising faster in the outside world. Thus great train robberies, pay van snatches and other notorious crimes demanding solution take up massive police manpower and resources that some technical forethought at the scene of the crime might have saved. Needless police time and effort are also expended in arresting harmless drunks, prostitutes, pornographers and homosexuals – a mighty army of victimless criminals that has been put into

uniform in relatively recent times through self-righteous recruitment by redundant religion and pusillanimous politics. As these
pathetic little cases are processed through police stations and the
courts, in the streets outside curbless crime of unquestioned
virulence and arbitrary outbreak ravages the community, creating an epidemic of neurosis and injustice to which only the
mediocracy is immune.

CHAPTER TWENTY-TWO

Prostrate Press

'Once the disappearance of a paper was like a bereavement; now it is just another loss of job opportunities. . . . Increasingly everything it writes up is ungrammatical, misspelt, ambiguous, malapropian, inaccurate, misprinted, transposed and sloppily subbed.'

Though it has, in certain countries, had recent moments of glory exposing corruption in high places, the press is a paste replica of the jewel it used to be. Once known as the Fourth Estate of the Realm, it has become a workshop of the communications industry if not a counter of show business. In cataloguing – without recognising – the rise of the mediocracy, it has become a part of it. Causes of its decay are both internal and external.

Throughout the nineteenth century the gradual elimination of 'taxes on knowledge' and the spread of literacy, photography and photographic reproduction were behind the rise of popular journalism and mass-circulation newspapers. Small-circulation quality papers could look to advertising revenue in a time of emergent admass to subsidise prices to the consumer. Premises, plant, newsprint and labour remained relatively inexpensive. Till well into the twentieth century entrepreneurs with modest capital and abundant vision could become 'press barons' unless retarded by undue moral or aesthetic scruples. Whatever the scruples of their successors, a much more discouraging prospect confronts them. Indeed, had it not been for the press barons' general commercial acumen, which led them into profitable diversification, more great newspapers would already have collapsed.

The press has known its share of bungled business. Perhaps it has suffered more than most industries from the managerial revolution. While editorials remain as capricious as ever, they are now created by anonymous leader-writers. With the replacement of press-baron autocracy by boardroom oligarchy that represents both hereditary privilege and successful sycophancy, the vision, the great crusading causes (well or ill conceived) and consistent editorial policies have largely vanished. And as the personal quality of papers and journals diminishes, so too does 'brand loyalty'. Once the disappearance of a paper was like a bereavement; now it is just another loss of job opportunities. In line with trends throughout the business world, even more conspicuous than declining readership loyalty is declining staff loyalty. From the boardroom to the printroom personnel are forever 'shopping around' for faster bucks or finer fringe benefits. More seriously, when they do stay with one paper the reason is more likely to be that they have discovered a 'soft touch' than a 'soft spot'. By industrial anarchy in a business peculiarly prone to union blackmail, through the constant variation of its product and its inability to sell tomorrow the surplus produced today, one of the least viable of all industries is most regularly stabbed by unreasonable pay demands or smothered by opulent featherbedding. Anxious about their own short-term instead of long-term future, mediocratic managements lack leadership and courage – let alone the cinematic ruthlessness attributed to them – to stand firm before ultimatum 'negotiations'. Yet it is to our oracular daily that we turn to discover how the nation can beat inflation, control unreasonable unions, improve the competence of slack employers and call politicians to task for insincerity.

Not all the press's problems are of its own making. The quality press has, with some notable exceptions, slumped with the decline and fall of the intellectual. Being particularly dependent on advertising revenue, it is vulnerable to downturns in the trading cycle; for, though the theory is that one should advertise more keenly when sales are low, most big corporations see prestige advertising as a luxury that can be afforded only when times are good. All types of press advertising, save classified and financial, are under pressure from commercial television, whether the economy is sound or not. Both 'public service' and commercial television offer information programmes that satisfy curiosity about the world and reduce time for serious reading, so most people are reducing the number of papers they buy, especially after price increases. Save in the Third World, which is still in a nineteenth-century phase of mounting literacy, the population explosion is not therefore producing a corresponding demand for newspapers. Not only is consumer resistance a serious limiting factor, but newsprint is growing scarcer and dearer. Derived chiefly from vegetation which is relatively slow-growing and land-hungry, and in rising demand for the prodigal packaging industry, paper is one product that has convincingly lined the ecological bandwagon. Still burnt rather than recycled, it has risen dramatically in price to become a major cost item in newspaper production. This has especially overtaken the popular, mass-circulation papers, which had always relied for their prosperity on low variable cost in relation to unit cost per thousand copies. The stage is now reached where advertising must sometimes be declined because of the cost of newsprint to carry it.

It is possible that these accumulated problems could have been overcome by an able, dedicated and constantly renewed workforce, sustained by regular injections of capital. In the many countries where the press is manipulated or controlled by the State, finance may be available but talent is not. Clever *apparatchiki* can find more satisfying, and infinitely safer, occupations with a higher reward/risk ratio. In countries with a 'free press' both money and talent are scarce. It is virtually impossible for an individual to establish a national daily today. Men with fire in their bellies and funds in their pockets are rare. If their place has been taken at all – and the tendency is for existing papers to die, not new ones to be born – it is by consortia of commercial conformists. One hundred years ago almost any able and determined journalist without private means but with the support of a voluntary society or local community behind him could found a journal. Even then there was a high mortality rate, but most of these papers had some sort of infancy and a few reached maturity. Their circulations were numbered in thousands, or even hundreds, but costs were so low they might be viable with specialist advertising revenue. Today such an undertaking is unthinkable. Journalists today must face the prospect of a lifetime as 'wage slaves', perhaps rising to the position of editor, where they daily look to directors, lawyers, accountants, advertising and circulation managers for their editorial line. Consequently, the profession has now little attraction for other than mediocrities, and a fair proportion of talent recruited in the past has already fled to the electronic media or public relations.

Happily, supply and demand are in perfect balance. A prostrate press is ministered to by a supine mediocracy.

Apart from employing its own mediocracy the press has richly supported mediocracy at large. Persuaded that 'the medium is the message', the underground press is quite undiscriminating over the words and pictures it uses, on the proven assumption that its product is bought (if at all) for what it 'represents' rather than what it contains, while the overground press reacts more cautiously. Probably holding the same views but lacking the courage of its convictions even in this, it has compromised with regular features and 'formula journalism'. Instead of sounding the humdrum of staff writers, which might at least have local colour, it syndicates the banalities of some internationally famous columnist. Naïve readers are agreeably surprised that the great man should write for an organ he might not have been expected to have heard of, while the publishers benefit from the economies of scale: syndicated notoriety is cheaper than original obscurity. What holds for feature columns is true of horoscopes, crossword puzzles, comic strips, recipes, gardening tips, fashion hints and other outpourings from an international mediocracy. Formula journalism, which is found particularly in the popular tabloids, is the trendy successor of political allegiance or philosophical outlook which once gave identity and continuity to the press. It has led to the 'woman's magazine', which presents as full and accurate a picture of the average woman as a swearing, screaming Women's Lib broadsheet; the 'sex magazine', whose only talent is to discriminate between the licentious and the unlicensed; the tabloid 'family' daily, which combines prurience with wayside pulpits, tits with tributes to chastity, and lovingly detailed mayhem with moral outrage. It has enabled politicians to gain considerable public sympathy when declaring 'the popular Press gets sillier, dirtier and more degraded than ever'[1] and makes the community less responsive to genuine journalistic *exposés*.

By its determination 'to put money into the pockets of criminals, charlatans, traitors, bent sportsmen, dissolute aristocrats and Kings of the Con Men',[2] ostensibly because their story will be a warning to the community, the press both glamorises delinquency and ensures that crime does pay. Charlatans and mini-martyrs, brawling sportsmen and ageing socialites, leaking

[1] Harold Macmillan, *At the End of the Day*, p. 438.
[2] E. S. Turner, 'Fifty Things Wrong with the Press', in *Punch*, 25 July 1973.

politicians and wet starlets all benefit from its free publicity. With its 'scare' headlines it exacerbates every crisis: runs on currency, stockmarket sellouts, hoarding scarce or threatened goods, war neurosis. And increasingly everything it writes up is ungrammatical, misspelt, ambiguous, malapropian, inaccurate, misprinted, transposed and sloppily subbed.

CHAPTER TWENTY-THREE

Blathering Broadcasting

*'Good broadcasters. . . . must be able to make the trivial important
and the important trivial. . . . Not only does the medium promote
mediocrities, it is itself mediocre. . . . Its universal commercialisation in the First World and universal politicisation in the Second
magnify these trends in society.'*

If there is any truth at all in the trendy slogan, 'the medium is the
message', it is that some media seem to lend themselves to some
sorts of message. Thus the electronic media – radio and television – are peculiarly suited to the values of an electronic age;
just as all mass media reflect both the oligarchy of admass and
the anarchy of the masses. Indeed, broadcasting is a perfect
example of how the rise of technology can co-exist with the
decline and fall of the intellectual, hereditary privilegentsias
with the rise of democracy, and the rise of bureaucracy with the
collapse of authority. Some corners of radio have managed to
stay 'hot' in media jargon, that is, to keep a place for logic,
intellectual argument, verbal felicity and the cultivation of the
imagination; but 'cool' television has become almost entirely a
vehicle for the disjunctive, anti-intellectual, gossipy and superficial.

Public broadcasting began with radio music – still its most
effective and valuable offering. When the spoken word was
added, the medium seemed unable to decide whether it should be
informative or diverting, an extension of newspapers or an extension of showbiz. This dichotomy has persisted, though the showbiz faction is gradually winning out. Its elevation has not meant
the elimination of bad news from news bulletins. On the con-

trary, doom has gained a more dominant place in blathering broadcasting than in newspapers; but it must be entertaining doom, tragedy with good sound effects, and televisual disaster. As a technological medium, broadcasting is devoted to sophisticated 'technique' and shares the fate of everything so devoted: it attracts unsophisticated technicians like iron filings round a magnet. This is as true of its 'creative' production staff as of its electricians and sound engineers.

Because its practitioners have no recognisable special talents and, in many countries, no recognised training schemes before selection, great emphasis is placed on 'professionalism'. This entails no selection by competitive examination or samples of work, no traditions of dedicated apprenticeship, no codes of professional ethics. The 'professional' broadcaster is more likely to be the presentable frontman of a clique or pressure group, or a relative of other broadcasters, than are professionals in any other way of life. He is a man with no particular knowledge save a smattering of electronics, no particular ability save a propensity for politicking, and no particular goal save to produce 'good radio' or 'good television'. He must know how to keep his programmes clean and his nose cleaner in the organisation that employs him. He should never be carried away by earnestness or originality or a taste for the subtle nuances of real life. Even more than press reporters and editors, good broadcasters must appear to know more about everyone else's job than he knows himself while being less able to ask a really incisive question than a clever schoolboy. They must be able to make the trivial important and the important trivial. If they cannot make the complex simple and the controversial trendy, they must keep to simpler subjects. If they cannot put the philosophy of ages into one or two sentences, or find a studio guest who can, they must avoid philosophy. Even if they work for religious broadcasting departments, they must not appear too religious; but it is even more damaging to appear irreligious. Similarly, they must not appear too establishmentarian in politics; but it is even more damaging to appear too liberal. In recent years it has become trendy to be an 'apolitical' supporter of every freedom fighter, hijacker, skyjacker, revolutionary, guerrilla, rioter and picketer, whatever cause each may represent, presumably on the grounds that bomb-throwing and rioting are 'good television' and violent language 'good radio', so long as the whole package of montage, sound-mixing, graphics and background music is attractively presented.

As the most pervasive medium in the world, broadcasting often claims to be the most influential. Ideological drivellers speak of 'participation' by the masses in the 'global village' it creates. When they are not denouncing it as the cause of murder and mayhem, rape and randiness, moralists speak of its aversive power, building up our revulsion against monstrous neo-colonial wars or corrupt presidents. It is supposed to be the cat's whisker in 'actuality' drama and the bee's knees in instantaneous news broadcasts. Yet even these claims are illusory. Not only does the medium promote mediocrities, it is itself mediocre. This is especially true of television. A television audience is usually as responsive and always as passive as a fistful of dough in a baker's hands. It is preached at and patronised, muddled and manipulated, titillated and irritated far from a global village or any other sort of village. For television is the most isolating and anti-social of media. It is also the most diminishing. Old films that hold one spellbound, beguiled, delighted or terrified in the dramatic caverns of a sound-drenched cinema lose their glamour, charm, hilarity or tension when reduced to the blurred and flickering visage of a mumbling box; while colour television turns the nuances of nature into gaudy glitter. Blinking and muttering in a living-room among talking visitors, however reprimanded, intrusive cats and chattering budgerigars, television invests every issue it raises with a droning monotony, deadening the senses and fraying moral fibre. Wars or corruption – we've seen it all before and shall see it all again, perhaps with added drama.

Unless it has a set-piece programme to beam by satellite round the world, television relies on film which is slower and more difficult to transport than the spoken or written word. Thus television news is always behind radio news and usually behind daily newspapers. Because it is a 'visual' medium it has other drawbacks. Seldom are the great moments of history – conference agreements, germinating thoughts in the minds of creative writers, hostilities or incidents that provoke declarations of war – made public at the time, much less posed before candid cameras. All that television presents is a Platonic image, often tarnished, of the real world but one which its producers hold in greater reverence than a whole galaxy of physical globes, and on which they endlessly ask celebrities to comment. Many of these celebrities are ageing refugees from other media or paragons of sport and showbiz who have no necessary expertise in theology, politics, economics or whatever else a television/radio mediocrat might throw at them. Considered as a newspaper, electronic news magazines benefit from the occasional power to catch out a public figure in some telltale hesitation, scowl or blush, but for the most part lack time to check out stories, honesty to publish corrections or wish to receive 'letters to the editor'.

Television is peculiarly given not only to finding its own mediocracy but to stimulating mediocracy at large. Its universal commercialisation in the First World and universal politicisation in the Second magnify these trends in society. Its trivialisation makes everything seem trivial. Its recent decision, in most countries, to limit any piece of speech to four minutes has made the four-minute dissertation as intrinsically incredible but now as commonplace as the four-minute mile, and given everyone the brains of birds and butterflies. By encouraging every rowdy and rioter to play up to the camera and glamorising every guerrilla, broadcasting has done much to increase our expectations of and deaden our sensitivity to violence in modern life, even when it is not guilty of fomenting chequebook demonstrations. In entertainment or information it is blindly 'committed to the second-rate. It is very largely either propaganda, with a bit of entertainment pushed into it, or pap, with a bit of news and current affairs pushed into it. The power of money and the power of government play upon broadcasting organisations all over the world. And this is what emerges all the time – that it is either pap or propaganda.'[1] Alternatively, it is either pap or pop. Because of relative expenditure and effort, very often 'the programmes are more boring than the commercials'.[2] Soon people come to accept the drabness of work and the colour of commercialism everywhere.

After half a century of noisy electronic mediocrity, people have lost their taste for the other arts. Painting, 'making music' with the family, quiet reading, good conversation, balanced entertaining, discussion circles, political and trade union meetings, lectures, poetry readings – all have declined with the rise of blathering broadcasting. Deprived of adequate advertising revenue and patronage from the *literati*, innumerable small,

[1] Joan Bakewell and Nicholas Garnham, *The New Priesthood: British Television Today*, London, 1970, pp. 228–9.
[2] Ibid., p. 168.

serious literary, political, religious or humanist journals have folded. Those books which broadcasting has promoted are usually glossy and meretricious, sensational and bogus. Perhaps the medium is, after all, influential, if only indirectly.

CHAPTER TWENTY-FOUR

Anarchic Architecture

'As building inspectors proliferate and town planners multiply, buildings become less safe and towns look less planned.... Innumerable committees, subcommittees and on-site consultations have produced the shapeless, featureless, dangerous, prematurely shabby and obsolescent monster overhead.'

Nothing more clearly demonstrates the capacity of a mediocracy to create problems while supposedly solving them, and the law of diminishing returns deriving from manifold unco-ordinated activity, than architecture since the eighteenth century. Nothing is more indebted to the rise of technology, bureaucracy and sociology. Nothing more clearly shows the capacity of these developments to employ both mediocrities and frustrated talent in the service of self-perpetuating mediocracy.

As the range and complexity of building materials are extended, visual impact is contracted. As the numbers of experts and subcontractors engaged in major construction projects grow, so too do the inadequacies of the end-product. As building inspectors proliferate and town planners multiply, buildings become less safe and towns look less planned. At the same time, local, regional, provincial and national variations that once reflected human diversity and individuality are being lost in a crude cosmopolitanism. Wherever one travels round the world today one finds the same malfunctioning 'functional' architecture; the same steel-concrete-glass tower blocks bizarrely overshadowing baroque squares or medieval terraces, mosques or marketplaces, pagodas or palaces; the same 'architect-designed' suburban boxes in humbugging brick veneer; the same 'spaghetti junctions' of flyovers and underpasses; the same interminable pedestrian walk-ways and subways leading nowhere in the sinuses of the air or the bowels of the earth; the same shopping precincts with the same plate-glass shops selling the same bric-à-brac at the same inflated prices.

As great wastes of shutter-scarred concrete testify to the cult of 'natural' surfaces, composition panels are made to look like marble, aluminium like brick, wallpaper like plaster (or leather or brocade) and plastics like wood. As with modern fabrics and simulated furs, nothing seems to consist of what it looks like or how it is described. It is as though decorators were overwhelmed by the problem of bigness in the range of options facing them. So too are the structural designers, with more serious consequences. Curtain-walling is sometimes designed with 'interlocking' panels which may lock together when the façade stays put and certainly lock together if it all tumbles down; alternatively, it is not uncommon for well-anchored curtain-walling to scatter bricks and bits of masonry on forecourts and pavements because while it consists of material that expands the building's framework consists of material that contracts. 'Luxury' offices resplendent in the last thing in tinted glass turn out to have wasteful heat loss in winter and stupefying heat gain in summer. Their ducts are full of inflammable plastic and when a fire breaks out on one floor it rapidly spreads to the top. If automatic sprinklers do not work at the point of outbreak, hand-operated fire extinguishers do not exist, cannot be found or are too complicated for laymen to manipulate. Supposedly pressurised internal stairwells, that work perfectly in all but the artificial conditions created by fire, have taken the place of 'unsightly' external fire-escapes. And this in a building whose height is grotesquely out of proportion to its breadth, whose entrance is unrelated to its façade, and whose skyline is a clutter of vents and engine-houses. One could readily be persuaded that modern buildings, like Topsy, 'just growed' did one not chance to see displayed outside during the construction stage a formidable board (or boards) recording not only a wealth of developers, finance companies, insurance offices, banks and assorted financial whizzkiddery, but whole firms of architects, quantity surveyors, structural, heating, lighting and ducting engineers, consultants, contractors and subcontractors, whose combined expertise and innumerable committees, subcommittees and on-site consultations have produced the shapeless, featureless, textureless, dangerous, prematurely shabby and

obsolescent monster overhead. So we find groups of noisy building workers and genteel conservationists lashing themselves to a
fury in campaigns to save some nineteenth-century eyesore on
the not unreasonable assumption that *anything* which takes its
place in an even more tasteless age is likely to be uglier and more
inhuman.

Once buildings were commissioned by abbots, bishops,
princes, merchant adventurers or tightly disciplined guilds, that
generally knew what they wanted and in any case employed an
architect who was his own designer and engineer, surveyor and
contractor: in short, a meritocratic dictator. It might seem – and
is often suggested – that the anarchy in contemporary architecture is a morbid eruption of *laissez-faire* capitalism. Yet any
householder who has wanted to glaze in a veranda, put up a
toolshed in his back garden or, in some areas, paint his front
door red, knows how much room for free enterprise is allowed
today. The monstrous constructions, highway grids and parking
lots (when cars are said to be obsolescent), piecemeal development and fractured skylines are taking place in a planners'
paradise. Local, regional, provincial and national instrumentalities are forever planning and countermanding one another's
plans. Our cities are patchworked with rival outline plans, pro-
visional, interim, short-range and long-range development orders
and zoning regulations. Slums caused by past jerrybuilding or
present poverty are insignificant compared with those attributable to 'planning blight'. Once the planners designate areas
for 'slum clearance', road widening, 'urban renewal' or re-
development, unlike the abbots, bishops, princes, merchants or
guilds of the past, they seem unable to enforce demolition or
finance rebuilding within a reasonable time; but their planning
and zoning orders discourage redecoration and repairs and virtually freeze buying and selling, so that areas which were previously shabby soon become positively slummy.

Whatever orders obtain, by various means, moral or immoral,
some developers manage to erect grandiose buildings in urban
wildernesses and thus pre-empt overall development options
when the surrounding land is eventually cleared. Indeed, the
whole system of public surveillance, private litigation and
endemic graft is not so much an index of the wickedness of the
capitalist system – though it may be wholly and is usually
partially that – as of the rise of democracy with a plethora of
elected representatives at various levels endowed with enough

power to subjugate the weak but not enough to curb the strong. Moreover, architects are only moderately sick members of the poisoned professions, still able, if they were allowed, to impose some harmony on building projects, but they are victims of democratic rejection of inspired dictatorship in favour of commonplace committees. Yet social workers complain of social problems, and sociologists record public dissatisfaction, arising from anarchic architecture and urban squalor, without the appearance of democratic participation or accountability.

The social problems of this situation are complex, perhaps conjectural. But there is enough solid evidence to cause disquiet. Highrise has come about largely through cost accountancy on the basis of site values, which in turn have skyrocketed in the slip-stream of the population explosion. It is the same phenomenon which has in this century caused multi-occupation of houses originally built, in the bad old days, for one family. 'Highrise neurosis', especially in young mothers, vandalism which wrecks lifts and maroons the aged or infirm in a flooded sky, suicides, landlord-tenant confrontations, *anomie* and the fragmentation of the extended family are among possible consequences of sky-scraper accommodation. Huge office blocks draw growing numbers of workers into city centres, saturating public transport and roads during commuter hours and further encouraging the centralisation that governments are trying to avoid. And, as cities grow unmanageably large, they grow more expensive to main-tain, more crime-prone and less able to retain reliable workers in essential services. In their search for economic growth through urbanisation, the planners have denuded our cities of adequate transport workers, doctors, nurses, hospital beds, teachers, class-room places, ambulance and fire services and police forces, for megalopolises are attractive chiefly for the very rich and the very poor, young unmarrieds and dropouts, drug addicts and the underworld. While, however, they do not cater for the average, they satisfy the mediocre and foment mediocrity.

CHAPTER TWENTY-FIVE

Arid Art

'Concern with "impressions" has since been used to justify the "vision" of charlatans, morons, maniacs, slapdashers, drug addicts and drunks. . . . The ethnologically unsuitable was joined in trendy ateliers *by the technologically unsuitable. . . . The general public . . . has turned its back, as far as it can, on the boundless desert of modern art.'*

Someone who has marched in the very front line of the *avant-garde* got to know an artist who bore arms beside him. 'His principal art was collage, done with brilliant scraps of cloth on plywood, in which – according to his own story – he started out to be a charlatan and became an artist in spite of himself.'[1] The world of art is rich in mavericks, and constantly evolving. Old artists are reassessed; new ones are tested. The charlatan-turned-artist 'was a visionary who saw the entire universe as a manifestation of light, and denounced Leonardo da Vinci and Rembrandt for bringing mud and grime into painting'. Those non-artists who still value Leonardo and Rembrandt (if there be any left) may feel that the world of modern art has been overtaken by visionaries who started out to be artists and became charlatans in spite of themselves, mingling with mystics who started out to be charlatans and succeeded triumphantly.

With the collapse of systems and authority and the rise of technology and neophilia, all the arts have abandoned the traditions of craftsmanship and apprenticeship, of exposition and revelation, of assimilation and transmission from which they grew. They seem now to have had no beginning and certainly to have no end. To talk of 'our cultural heritage' is to invite contempt, if

[1] Alan Watts, *In My Own Way*, pp. 318–19.

not certification. Even among the fuddy-duddies there are few who want fossilised art or deny the need for experimentation. But experimentation is, by their definition, a trying out, a testing of experience and techniques to develop the *data* of human history and potentiality, to reach out to dimly glimpsed goals, to separate the adventitious and expendable from the abiding and valuable, to find improved means of communicating one's vision to those who will make some effort of concentration. Not so among modernists. To them experimentation expresses their contempt for the past, for tradition, for skill, for intelligence, for elucidation, for communication. It begins as liberation from the past and ends as bondage to the eternally trendy.

To the general public 'modern' painting connotes Impressionism, which is already a century old and an extension of experimentation by Constable and Turner in the early nineteenth century. Now the Impressionists are anathema to the *avant-garde* for what they did, which is representational, precise and painterly, though concern with 'impressions' has since been used to justify the 'vision' of charlatans, morons, maniacs, slapdashers, drug addicts and drunks. Other trends began to flow in the nineteenth century into the mighty flood we have today. The spread of empire and rise of sociology exposed the artistic community in every country to a range of alien styles and art-forms whose traditions and true significance were but dimly discerned and whose main appeal was their novelty. Coupled with the Gothic Revival this influence promoted the cult of the 'primitive', where naïvety passed for simplicity and sloppiness for naturalism. With the rise of technology came a bewildering range of new materials, so that in many cases the ethnologically unsuitable was joined in trendy *ateliers* by the technologically unsuitable.

In the twentieth century disintegration graduated from the status of a fact to the status of a cult. Aided by political chaos resulting from two world wars and intellectual chaos resulting from the popularity of psychoanalysis and existentialism, wilful subjectivism became the only artistic yardstick. Uncurbed by rational criticism or professional objectivity, the art world passed rapidly from Fauvism via Cubism, Expressionism, Futurism, Abstractionism and Vorticism to Dada, Surrealism and Constructivism. Terrified lest, like Ruskin, they should eventually be ridiculed for accusing a Whistler of throwing a pot of paint in the public's face, even those art critics independent of the international art market cheered as artists began throwing – or dribbling, stamping, rolling or cycling – paint on their canvases or boards, under the inspiring banner of abstract expressionism, tachism or action painting. That some of these pictures consisted of bubbles of car enamel and aluminium paint unstably facing swathes of oil paint was disregarded. Pundits were soon pointing out that Leonardo's egg tempera was also unstable and were ready to justify comparable prices. While wishing to be paid as if their work were potentially marketable and permanent, since the Second World War some artists have directed their attention to the 'unmarketable' and the 'instantaneous'. These have taken many forms: the staging of sundry 'events' and 'happenings', which may be recorded for posterity on film or, better, for semi-posterity on cheaper videotapes with a life of some 100 hours; the use of deliberately disintegrating materials for 'destruction-in-art'; the grandiose ephemera of 'conceptual' art.

Today, as we step into expensively constructed, decorated, air-conditioned and lit art galleries all over the world, we find second-rate cosmopolitan imitations of the mediocre enlivened by 'special exhibitions' financed by some arts council, foundation or tax-avoidance trust. As these will contain a fair proportion of 'readymades' like bricks, bicycle wheels and toilet seats isolated by the discerning eye of the artist, it is not always immediately apparent what constitutes the exhibits and what the architecture of the establishment or the personal possessions of its attendants. Apart from survivors of the twentieth-century schools previously named and neophiliac variants like neoprimitivism, neodada and neorealism, the art objects that are clearly exhibits will consist of: pop art, combining wisps of paint with press cuttings, tele-grams, photographs and silk-screen prints of commercial wrappers and posters of pop stars; op art's meagre offering of optical illusions; collages of acrylic, sand, soil and anything that might be found in the average housewife's workbox or domestic garbage can; funk art, sounding surrealistic alarms from draw-ings, ceramics, contrivances and sculptures whose forms are so precariously balanced they are positively dangerous to the beholder; minimal art, which reduces the whole world of experience to a few geometric shapes; post-minimal art, which further reduces it up to consummation in an utterly blank canvas; 'the void', which is empty of purpose in being empty. As one walks around, taking care not to let clothing get caught in various clunking or coughing electronically operated mobiles, one may bump against erratically moving human figures who turn out to be 'living sculptures', presumably submitted to the hanging committee by the Almighty, before coming upon a television lounge. Here, on videotape or closed-circuit television, one may see the more circumscribed offerings of conceptual art – people sitting nude, eating, drooling, laughing, weeping – or body art, where they play with themselves, plaster themselves with entrails, clamp paper clips to themselves, pull out their pubic hairs, or burn themselves. Interested spectators are referred to the untrammelled world of conceptual art outside, to creative artists drawing random patterns with sticks on sand-dunes, wrapping whole headlands in brown paper and – for those who like the challenge of intractable materials – sculpting water. If one is lucky enough to join the artistic, political and philanthropic establishment at the official opening, one may happily join, by courtesy of taxpayers or ratepayers, junketings like time-tabled streaking, happenings staged by celebrated barbarians or the ritual electrocution and barbecuing of catfish in tanks.

It is hardly surprising that the general public, always suspicious of 'art for art's sake', has turned its back, as far as it can, on the boundless desert of modern art. The separation is not complete, for the foyers and forecourts of contemporary buildings boast monstrous shapes in stainless steel and plexiglass, cast iron and plastic, to educate the man-in-the-street in new awareness and enhanced sensibility. Within the artistic world there were, for a time, middle-aged schoolboys who pointed ignorant fingers and spoke of the emperor's new clothes, but the full weight of money and mediocracy has borne them down. A consortium of dealers and collectors, private gallery owners and public gallery curators, art critics and art consultants, speaks in a shout that cannot be drowned. Once they were confined to authentic old masters (and tolerable forgeries), but they have recently learnt how to manipulate the output of the living. In the field of antiques a kindred consortium has discovered how to relate demand to supply, has brought under the umbrella of antiques *kitsch* Edwardiana or *vertu* of later vintage, and has made more plentiful and tasteless Victoriana more valuable than rarer and choicer Georgian pieces. Though the most successful of modern artists have seldom been hostile to materialism, they have usually sold their works for a fraction of resale value and their widows may well have fared worse than their executors, who often have links with international galleries. If the artists' tastes are simple, they may not need much output to pay the rent, but increasingly they are forming unions, consulting lawyers and accountants and forming companies to try to get a lick of the cream. In either case, professional artists tend to be too dispirited or too engaged in high finance to produce many paintings.

Life at the top is reflected at the bottom. Ambitious young art students soon discover that the road to riches is not paved with good drawing, draughtsmanship and colour-mixing, and that if they do not worship the intellectually and visually arid they will finish up putting pastels in the hands of troublesome teenagers or designing sets for detergent commercials. Art critics know that if they wish to become art consultants to wealthy collectors, dealers and curators, or even retain their jobs as critics, they must master the regulation prose where every banality 'transcends reality' and every monstrosity 'penetrates to the heart of human experience, laying bare its disturbing dichotomy, and metamorphoses inert matter into the magic of controlled energy'. Those who hold the purse strings of arts councils, educational institutions and art foundations have committed, or inherited the commitment of, so much cash to inflated artistic values that they are as horrified as private collectors by the likely consequences of any radical reappraisal. So it never occurs. Artistic charlatans and mediocrities not only prosper, but form an impregnable mediocracy. Like property and funny-money speculators they are, moreover, largely a mediocracy which could contribute to social disruption in times of political reaction. For 'modern art' is largely the expression of 'artists (or businessmen) in exile', unfortunately vulnerable to the charge of being a 'rootless cosmopolitan' minority, traditionally hostile to representational art and determined to foist their own personal tragedies and insecurity on society and civilisation at large.

CHAPTER TWENTY-SIX

Mangled Music

'There is almost total breakdown in communications between serious professionals and intelligent laymen. . . . This revival of the sentimentalia of yesteryear expresses a great human hunger for music that is not only intelligible but pleasant to listen to.'

From the *ars nova* of the fourteenth century, music has constantly been renewing itself in conscious rebellion against tradition. Despite biblical accounts of the use of instruments, Clement of Alexandria declared his opposition to the use of anything but the human voice, while Athanasius demanded minimal melody in the chants. *Ars nova* represented a shocking liberation of intervals, rhythms and instrumentation. With baroque music in the seventeenth century came another wave of 'new music' which enshrined improvisation and led to new forms like opera, oratorio, cantata, fugue, sonata, suite and concerto. At every new stage there were misgivings.

In the world of the arts, the French Revolution's *coup de grâce* to the Enlightenment and the Age of Reason took the form of replacement of classicism by romanticism, with interest in emotion, individuality and mystery. While it produced composers who have long been darlings of the concert hall, many of them caused fury in their own lifetimes occasioned as much by their personalities as by their compositions. Especially is this true of Wagner, whose *Tannhäuser* caused a riot and whose greatest admirer, King Ludwig II of Bavaria, was mad. Twentieth-century 'new music' is described as being anti-romantic, centring on impressionism, atonalism and neoclassicism, though it is rich in mediocratic variations of emotion, individuality and mystery. Impressionism, which began with Debussy in the late nineteenth century, was the first attempt to slice through romantic lushness to the core of musical structure and suggestiveness. Influenced by the decline of systems and authority, the atonalists and neo-classicists sought to escape the tyranny of the diatonic scale, and the operatic farce of tubercular deathbed scenes in opulent coloratura. But, as in other aspects of life, what began as interesting, if controversial, departures by gifted composers thoroughly grounded in traditional concepts and techniques soon turned to anarchy or narrower tyrannies. The flexible diatonic scale yielded to inflexible dodecaphonic, or serial, music. Polyphony and harmony were rejected in favour of the stridency of *musique concrète,* and people paid large sums and sat solemnly in concert halls to hear the sort of discord anyone without musical training could create on his own untuned piano or the flat vocalisation he could reproduce in his own bathtub.

Music has been so mangled one might even expect to hear it played on a mangle. Certainly washboards have joined cowbells and more familiar orchestral sounds in the symphonies of the *avant-garde.* When all conventional forms and instrumentation had been swept away, modern composers turned on the 'Western tradition' of time. Musical development and variations were abandoned as horizontal strands of music were used vertically. With the rejection of time, however, rhythm, tempo and melody (or anti-melody) also lost their *raison d'être* and compositions became a complete jumble of sound. Mercifully they were likely to be shorter. They lasted, alas, long enough to wreak havoc on concert grand pianos, whose strings were required to be muted, plucked, banged and assaulted in other ways not envisaged by their makers. In truly 'freaked out' concerts this damage did not matter for the pianist, in a final *jeu d'esprit,* took an axe to his crippled instrument. This was also a means of existentialist liberation for the tortured ears of his audience. Another came with the metaphysical discovery that analysis of music was really the pursuit of pure sound, and this is created not in a concert hall but inside the brain. So a contemporary composer, said to be 'an extremely accomplished musician' as well as a trend-setter, made the final musical leap. A friend has recorded the splendour of the event:

It was, as I remember, through Jean – who is to dancing what Vivaldi was to music – that we met the other member of the party, composer John Cage, who had then become interested in the relationship of music to Zen and was beginning to explore the melodies of silence. My principal tie with John was that we had the same kind of humour, for he would simply bubble with laughter whenever describing his latest plans for a musical outrage, such as a very formal piano recital in full evening dress, complete with an assistant to turn the pages, in which, however, the score consisted entirely of rests. The joke wasn't merely that he was getting away with murder in the hopelessly deranged world of *avant-garde* music, so as to constitute the master charlatan of all, but that beyond all this and to make matters still funnier, he had also discovered and wanted to share the meditation process of listening to silence.[1]

Knowing or caring nothing about Zen, sober music critics sat among elegant concert-goers going over in their minds the ecstasies of purple prose with which they would greet the performance on the morrow. For, mindful of how many new departures of the past had graduated from rejection to homage, and terrified of being thought fuddy-duddy, they were more than ready to attune themselves to anything.

It is no doubt folly to consider popular music separately, for the same critics have equated pop stars with Beethoven in artistic terms – though they would probably give an edge to pop because of its coverage. Canons of cultivated taste come and go but pop goes tritely on for ever. There is no reason to assume that it was, on average, better in the fourteenth than in the twentieth century; though within our own period it seems to be in decline. The musical comedy of a generation ago has borrowed from the formlessness, monotony and cacophony of 'serious' music to become the musical of today. Through electronic amplification pop music has gained an intensity of expression which is literally deafening, as if to make up in decibels what it lacks in melody; or, as 'mood music', modern blues and musical wallpaper, whines endlessly, pointlessly and self-indulgently on. With the rise of democracy pop has become big business, offering great fortunes to those who feature at the top of the charts or are plugged on mass-audience radio and television shows. Inevitably, a venal mediocracy of singers, songwriters, theatrical agents, record promoters,

1 Alan Watts, *In My Own Way*, p. 231.

production managers, producers and prostitutes has featured in chart-rigging and payola scandals. Whatever may be the abstract value of public opinion, when everything is mediocre, non-musical factors – even if as innocent as luck – must separate the subway busker from the superstar.

In so far as we can peer through the murk of admass to the real wishes of ordinary people, we discern reactions alarming for cultural development. For the first time there is almost total breakdown in communications between serious professionals and intelligent laymen. Save for the ritual radical-chic occasion, our concert halls, opera houses and cathedrals are given over almost entirely to works fifty years or more old, in an unprecedented rejection of contemporaries. This is not, as modern composers moan, through a conspiracy of impresarios and precentors, most of whom positively force a sprinkling of contemporary works on their audiences. In the world of light music, revivals of shows from the sugary twenties do infinitely better than the latest erotic musical. Even in the realm of pure pop, teenagers are more likely to whistle something from the thirties or forties – which also had a good sprinkling of slick lyrics – than the inchoate caterwauling of today. This revival of the sentimentalia of yesteryear expresses a great human hunger for music that is not only intelligible but pleasant to listen to. But teenagers are vaguely embarrassed by this return to the past, just as chanting natives in the Third World are embarrassed by ubiquitous tourists, and it is rare now to find people whistling or singing at their work. But music has not gone out of their lives. They have their transistors.

CHAPTER TWENTY-SEVEN

Lacklustre Literature

'Educational syllabus-setters . . . see contemporary poetry as the flashy, trashy, mish-mashy output of the "poetry circuit" and trendy publishers. . . . Readers gain added frisson *if the author is himself disreputable, drunken, addicted or delinquent. . . . Literary criticism . . . has endorsed every new departure, enshrined every cult and magnified every mediocrity.'*

While it is less plagued by locusts than the other arts, the field of literature is so overgrown by weeds as to be scarcely more productive. They have drawn nourishment from the rise of technology, bureaucracy and sociology, have been sheltered by the rise of democracy and have escaped weeding through the decline and fall of the intellectual. From the grassroots of literature, language itself has grown lank and rank.

It is rather the same thing that is happening to the English language. It becomes ugly and inaccurate because our thoughts are foolish, but the slovenliness of our language makes it easier for us to have foolish thoughts. The point is that the process is reversible. . . . A bad usage can spread by tradition and imitation, even among people who should and do know better.[1]

The book trade is overwhelmed by commercialism, the electronic revolution and the problem of bigness. By comparison with a hundred years ago, when mass literacy began, intimate forms of expression, not all of them to be mourned, are dying or dead: poems, serious novels, short stories, essays, *belles-lettres*

[1] George Orwell, 'Politics and the English Language' (*Horizon*, April 1946), in *The Collected Essays, Journalism and Letters of George Orwell*, London, 1968, Vol. IV, *In Front of Your Nose 1945–1950*, pp. 128 and 137.

and published sermons. Their place has been taken by textbooks, 'how to' books, coffee-table books, sensationalia and escapist fiction in hardcover, limpback, paperback or boxes, all packaged like convenience foods. As property values soar and space becomes more precious, books must be turned over quickly or pulped. As newsagents and supermarkets scoop the cream off the trade, the traditional bookshop with its extensive stock, ordering facilities and personal service is disappearing, and with it books for discriminating readers. Mass-produced coffee-table books based on little editing and less research, and reprints of out-of-copyright classics are sold so cheaply and remaindered so frequently the buying public has a totally false notion of the economics of publishing original work of limited appeal. Even so, a good book sells for about the price of a night out at a good restaurant, but the cultivated world has a new sense of values in evening enrichment. Driven by necessity and increasingly, one suspects, with the decline and fall of the gentleman publisher, by taste, publishers are cost-accounting their titles, streamlining their publicity and 'hitting' the market with instant books. At best these are good journalism; at worst, frenzied ventilation of the bogus, drearily written, rarely read, but bought, dipped into, spoken about and prominently displayed.

Since the indexer, illustrator or jacket-designer – to say nothing of the editor, printer or bookshop assistant – may well earn more from a serious book than its author, primary writers are deserting the field of biography, history, philosophy, sociology and other 'heavy' non-fiction. Where reinforcements are needed they are recruited from academic writers on fat salaries and lush research grants, who pepper the air with extended bibliographies and scant regard for fine writing, or even grammar. Books they regard as an extension of their involvement in lucrative lecturing and presiding over seminars, where typically 'scholarship was mixed with socializing and politicking ... witty reorganization of most familiar information' eliciting 'the kind of applause ... giving me the feeling that people were judged by reputation rather than substance'.[1] Unfortunately these tendencies are well marked within the fastnesses of Eng. Lit. itself, whose textbooks are as ponderous, plagiaristic, imprecise and uninspired as any others.

Confronted by publishing empires where smaller houses may

[1] Yen Yuan-shu, 'Is comparative literature to be all-Western?', in *Free China Weekly* (Taipei), 23 December 1973.

have 'remained as mere imprints within group companies' that show 'impersonality, rigidity, committee decisions, the usual complaints', writers turn to agents hoping them to be 'more powerful and sophisticated'.[1] Powerful, perhaps; sophisticated, hell. These gross ten-per-centers, who live well off literary estates and do not want the bother of living authors (though they will make exceptions for bestseller barons), show greater facility in drawing cheques for themselves than drawing up watertight contracts for their clients, who increasingly do their own promotion and conduct all delicate negotiations with their publishers.

The area of 'creative writing' has become a jungle which would be intolerable for creative writers did they not show growing alacrity to wear loincloths. Further, like natural jungles, it is a dwindling territory. Despite neophilia and vulgarianism, regular appeals to the working classes and pretensions to spiritual and moral uplift proportional to counter-claims of depravity and corruption, it has largely been rejected by educated laymen, who would, with some justification, gladly settle for seventeenth-century drama, eighteenth-century criticism and nineteenth-century verse and fiction. At least in verse, much good writing is still appearing, but it is in inaccessible places unfrequented by educational syllabus-setters and anthologisers, who see contemporary poetry as the flashy, trashy, mish-mashy output of the 'poetry circuit' and trendy publishers, and give it an understandably wide berth. Certainly in the West and probably in the East, 'people's theatre' is patronised not by the workers but by the middle classes, despite – or perhaps because of – its passion for working-class values and language. As with the visual, so with the literary arts, artists themselves have greatly contributed to the devaluation of art.

> But just as creating is a natural impulse, so it's just as natural to hear, see or read what is produced. I mean, a woman in the street explaining to a neighbour what happened to her last night is art at its most basic and crude level. Both the gossip and the 'gossiped-to' are eager participants.[2]

Some artists would go further into 'street theatre', proclaiming the gossip's art as the loftiest and noblest of all.

If the generality of literature is lacklustre, dulled by the

[1] *The Economist*, London, 10 November 1973.
[2] Trevor Philpot, 'Wesker's World', in *New Humanist*, July 1974.

dullards who surround it, its *avant-garde* glows in the glitter of mediocratic gadflies. Many of them are far from being mediocrities, but years of neglect in traditional fields have made them ready to jump fences for any travelling circus, or improvise trapeze acts of their own. Unfortunately, their confinement to sundry sawdust rings and animal cages instead of the open spaces of literature brings all the cramped artificiality but none of the discipline that usually goes with circuses.

Biography has become instant accounts, genuine or fraudulent, of the luridness of notorieties or rehashed versions of the lives of notabilities. Pioneered by Lytton Strachey – whose celebrity, like that of other cult figures of the last hundred years, is inversely proportional to his actual output – bitchiness is the dominant characteristic of works about the truly great; while sycophancy licks the feet of the second-rate. Broadly, the novel may be classified as introverted or extroverted. One type tends to be an unappetising broth of ill-digested Freud and Dostoevsky; the other, a distillate of personal adventures. Typical of the psychological novel is existentialist exploration of perversion and the *acte gratuit*. In a world where social barriers are breaking down and invention is at a discount, readers gain added *frisson* if the author is himself disreputable, drunken, addicted or delinquent. Indeed, in one supposedly cultured country the literary establishment is said to be an extension of the underworld. The 'adventure' novel also comes less from the imagination of a meritocrat than from the experiences of a mediocrat in war or cold war. Great reputations have been made from minimal involvement with the International Brigade during the Spanish Civil War, or moments of guts and glory in the Second World War, or 'intelligence' work then or since. Literary lives increasingly peak with first novels and graduate to lingering anticlimax.

In the theatre we see the steady disappearance of the proscenium arch, period costume, clothes, poetry, plot and logical dialogue – elements showing varying degrees of artistic expendability. One modern playwright has admitted that the great repute he earned when young for fractured dialogue, said by critics to represent failure of communication and inner loneliness in the modern world, largely resulted from lack of verbal facility. In the truly *avant-garde* theatre there may be no dialogue at all. Performers shout insults at audiences, sometimes shut up in cages to enhance the dramatic experience, and copulate with or without audience participation. While purity crusaders agonise over public morals and public decency, 'the distinctive feature of our erotic theatre is not its extent, nor its outspokenness, nor its survival despite the legal restrictions – but its rather poor quality.'[1] When it is not a slavish imitation of classical traditions, ballet also falls victim to lightweight experimentation, while the *libretti* of modern operas accord perfectly with their music. But perhaps the most depressing literary decline in the last hundred years is that of poetry.

Two hundred years ago poets were the cronies of aristocrats, if they were not aristocrats themselves. One hundred years ago they were the pop stars of the bourgeoisie. Today, through a combination of social forces and personal wilfulness, their only celebrity is a twilight flicker on selected university campuses. Contemporary poetry

> peeps slyly between the spaces left in the highbrow weeklies after the political articles, the reviews, and the advertisements have been set up in type; it rampages in public before huge audiences, sometimes to the sound of music; it is, in a British writer's phrase, 'a modest art'; it is used as a political weapon, to ban bombs and drive the American forces from Vietnam. The situation of contemporary verse is confused and contradictory; on the one side a battlefield, on the other a drawing-room, and both are strewn with old manifestos.[2]

Since the relative importance of the *avant-garde* rises as the total impact of culture falls, so poetry has assumed a progressive waywardness. In pursuit of 'feeling' it has become mindless and in pursuit of 'liberation' formless. Rhyme and rhythm began the exodus of every traditional feature of verse, till only words were left: slabs or jumbles of words 'found' (and sounding better when described in French as *vers trouvé*) in legal documents or telephone directories, or arranged in symbolic patterns on the page as concrete verse or poster poems. But why should words be sacrosanct when they are only the vehicle of feeling? So they were broken down to their component letters or phonemes and 'typewriter' and 'sound' poetry were born. What interest these novelties convey has less to do with literature than with visual art, music and sociology.

The creative world of modern literature has been well served

1 John Elsom, *Erotic Theatre*, London, 1973, p. 253.
2 Jonathan Raban, *The Society of the Poem*, London, 1971, p. 9.

by literary criticism. This has endorsed every new departure, enshrined every cult and magnified every mediocrity. Being poorly paid and published in cramped corners of a dwindling number of periodicals, its practitioners often feel justified in reviewing a book after reading the publisher's blurb and the first and final pages, and a play after seeing the first act. Superficial reviewing lends itself to the reviewing of superficial works; sensational, sensational; standardised, standardised; cheap and nasty, nasty and cheap.

CHAPTER TWENTY-EIGHT

Filmic Flotsam

'The charismatic star of yesteryear has been supplanted by "the boy/girl next door", who can be seen more cheaply next door. . . . If psychologically disposed one may be entertained by public urination, defaecation, vomiting, fellatio *and* pedicatio, *sometimes by performers whose equipment is as mediocre as their talents.'*

In its short history the cinema seems, like a lanky teenager, to be forever growing out of its clothes. Ideally, it is a unique blend of all the arts; practically, it is far less satisfactory. From its inception it has been self-conscious about technique and the first film producers were engineers rather than artists, willing to shoot anything to show off their new toy. For a time there was a reversal of this trend with the arrival of the first full-length features as filmed plays, but then cinematic technique took over again, starting with Hollywood's silent comedies. These comedies were, on the whole, economy productions shot *al fresco* or in converted barns before fixed cameras, and the techniques used were a combination of engineered stunts and optical illusions grafted on to tricks of the circus clown. It is a little ironic that they are today so fashionable with intellectuals, since they were mostly non-intellectual or anti-intellectual to a degree. Their immense charm and popularity derive from their spontaneity, simplicity and, in the finest examples, portrayal of basic human emotions. When some of their stars have, in later life, attempted more sophisticated themes and treatments they have usually been disasters. Indeed, contemporary enthusiasm for these early comedies is generally a comment on their successors rather than a just appraisal of the original works. For it is clear they had two advantages conspicuously lacking in many recent productions: their stars were mostly graduates of music halls, where they had served long and exacting apprenticeships, and prodigiously hard workers in the film industry; unity of production and direction gave a sense of artistic unity often lacking in the products of committee compromises.

While new techniques have made possible the achievement of new emotional experiences – for example, shock and revulsion – and some films have been thoughtful, or even propagandist, the medium is overwhelmingly escapist. Thus there has developed another special cult among film buffs, who tend to be *aficionados* of everything: the 'golden years of Hollywood' in the thirties and forties. Though not, on the whole, valued highly at the time, and often denounced for seeming oblivion to depression and war, in retrospect films of this period glow with the true colours of escapism in their star-quality stars, lavish sets, catchy tunes, strong story lines and happy endings. Many of their successors contrive to be neither thought-provoking nor entertaining, neither actual nor magical. Instead of glamour we have squalor. The charismatic star of yesteryear has been supplanted by 'the boy/girl next door', who can be seen more cheaply next door, the forgettable 'superstar' of the underground cinema and the 'method' actor whose mumblings are almost unintelligible. Tuneful or romantic scores, which had no lasting value, have given way to noisy electronic effects which often have no value at all. With the *nouvelle vague*, plots have become incomprehensible puzzles or meaningless meanderings, interesting at first as a reflection of the lives of a certain class of dropout or hippie-anarchist or minor playboy, but not gaining by repetition and imitation. The unreality of happy endings and wholesome themes has yielded to the unreality of the pornographic skin-flick. Though the underground cinema, or filmic 'conceptual' art, has undermined dubious conventions, artistic and moral, and intolerable censorship, it is memorable more by what it represents than by what it achieves. Among its soporific themes have been skyscrapers, empty rooms, ticking clocks, sunlight and sleep itself, lasting anything from twenty-four minutes to twenty-four hours. Closely related to 'underground' are 'experimental' films, whose prime concern seems to be with technique and which tend to be just as tedious though rather better shot.

That the film is the vehicle of the best light and popular music composed today is a tribute not to the richness of modern music but to its poverty. A greatly reduced film output in the First World manages to stretch mediocratic talents. This reduction has come about by many forces: the rise of the electronic media, especially television; the greater profitability of bingo in cinema; the high price of admission for what was once family entertainment. Though the cinema's technical origins are still less than a hundred years away, already it seems to be in a *Götterdämmerung*. One well-known modern director, who began as a film critic, openly speaks of its glories as past and shamelessly imitates bygone idioms. Moreover, a famous veteran 'was happier before sound came in because I thought they were truer motion pictures then'.[1]

Perhaps the most remarkable aspect of the film industry, and one showing most clearly the rise of the mediocracy, is the film festival. This takes many forms. There is the buffs' festival of impeccable directorial names and sometimes little else. There is the award-conferring festival of commercialism, razmataz and determinedly *décolleté* and predatory starlets. And there is the 'underground' festival, whose razmataz may be no less conspicuous. Among its attractions are the ultimate in 'experimentation' and sensationalia: mixed-media and transmedia events and 'happenings'. If psychologically disposed one may be entertained by public urination, defaecation, vomiting, *fellatio* and *pedicatio*, sometimes by performers whose equipment is as mediocre as their talents. Stages are wrecked, animals are tortured and one may be lucky enough to see a man decapitate a goose and stuff himself with the stump of its neck.

A modern critic has said that the Visigoths are at the gate. Once, no doubt, they were. Now, however, they are well inside, spewing on the bedclothes, leaking in the cooking pots, shitting on the hearth and fucking the master and the mistress.

[1] Peter Bogdanovich, *Allan Dwan: the last pioneer*, London, 1971, p. 104.

Index

For Product Safety Concerns and Information please contact our EU
representative GPSR@taylorandfrancis.com
Taylor & Francis Verlag GmbH, Kaufingerstraße 24, 80331 München, Germany

www.ingramcontent.com/pod-product-compliance
Lightning Source LLC
Chambersburg PA
CBHW062028270326
41929CB00014B/2356

9 781032 890142